PRAISE FOR *THE* MONA LISA *VANISHES*

WINNER OF THE ROBERT F. SIBERT MEDAL
WINNER OF THE BOSTON GLOBE–HORN BOOK AWARD

"A witty thriller."
—*The New York Times*

★ "A completely engaging book."
—*Booklist*, starred review

★ "Wildly entertaining!"
—*Publishers Weekly*, starred review

★ "Readers will love the brouhaha."
—*Kirkus Reviews*, starred review

———◇———

A *Publishers Weekly* Best
Book of the Year

A *School Library Journal*
Best Book of the Year

A *Kirkus Reviews*
Best Children's
Book of the Year

A *Bulletin*
Blue Ribbon Book

A *Booklist* Editors' Choice

An NPR "Books We Love"
Selection

A New York Public Library
Best Book for Children

A Chicago Public Library
Best of the Best Book

An ALA-ALSC Notable
Children's Book

RANDOM HOUSE STUDIO
NEW YORK

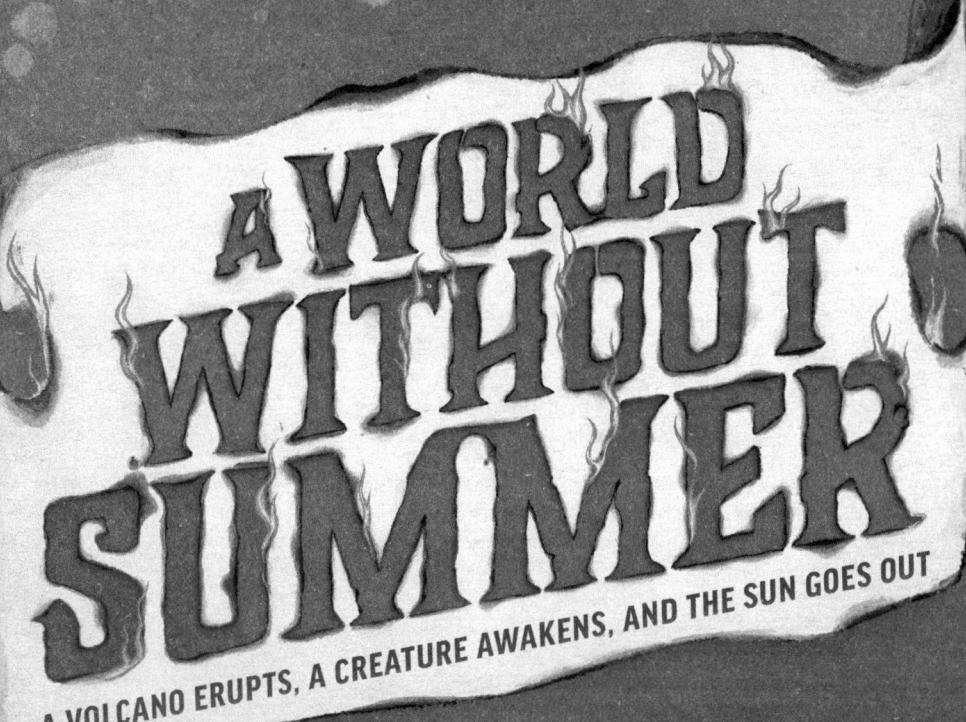

A WORLD WITHOUT SUMMER

A VOLCANO ERUPTS, A CREATURE AWAKENS, AND THE SUN GOES OUT

NICHOLAS DAY

WITH ART BY YAS IMAMURA

Random House Studio
An imprint of Random House Children's Books
A division of Penguin Random House LLC
1745 Broadway, New York, NY 10019
penguinrandomhouse.com
GetUnderlined.com

Library of Congress Cataloging-in-Publication Data is available upon request.
ISBN 978-0-593-64387-7 (trade) — ISBN 978-0-593-64388-4 (lib. bdg.) —
ISBN 978-0-593-64389-1 (ebook)

The artist used digital brushes and gouache to create the illustrations for this book.
The text of this book is set in 12-point Sabon LT Pro.
Parchment art by Peekeedee/stock.adobe.com
Ink wash art by PaperArcade/shutterstock.com and Shedesign/shutterstock.com
Interior design by Jade Rector

Manufactured in the United States of America
10 9 8 7 6 5 4 3 2 1

The authorized representative in the EU for product safety and compliance
is Penguin Random House Ireland, Morrison Chambers, 32 Nassau
Street, Dublin D02 YH68, Ireland, https://eu-contact.penguin.ie.

To A

−N.D.

To Dan

−Y.I.

CONTENTS

IT WAS A WARNING 1

PART I

FIRE AND FURY.. 7

    THE GODS WOULD RISE UP.................................... 9

    THE WORLD TURNED TO BURNING ASH 15

    A NATURAL EXPERIMENT....................................34

    SOME QUESTIONS FOR THE READER, ALSO KNOWN AS YOU, PART I......38

PART II

A DEATH AND A BIRTH 43

    A COMET IN THE SKY 45

RED SKIES AND RED SNOW 51

    A FEEDBACK LOOP OF BAD 53

    IT WAS A SIGN 58

THUNDER ROLLED DOWN THE YEAR 65

SOME QUESTIONS FOR THE READER,
ALSO KNOWN AS YOU, PART II 70

A LIFE WITHOUT COMPROMISE 73

SNOW AND SCANDAL 75

FROZEN FEET AND FROZEN BIRDS........................ 81

WHAT IS TO BECOME OF THIS COUNTRY 83

HOPES FELL FAST.................................... 87

MANY WRONGS DO NOT MAKE A RIGHT 91

THE FIRST WRONG 93

THE SECOND WRONG 97

THE THIRD WRONG.................................. 99

THE MANY, MANY, MANY OTHER WRONGS.............. 101

AND A RIGHT 103

SOME QUESTIONS FOR THE READER, ALSO KNOWN AS YOU, PART III ... 107

SOME ATE SOIL.. 109

CLAY AND CHOLERA.................................. 111

BREAD OR BLOOD 117

WE MUST HAVE FLOUR CHEAPER...................... 119

THIS EXTRAORDINARY TERROR 127

THE SPARK OF LIFE ITSELF 131

A HIDEOUS PHANTASM 133

I HAD THOUGHT OF A STORY 140

A GOOD YEAR FOR DREAD **143**

A VERY SHORT LIST OF WHAT GREW IN EUROPE IN 1816 . . . . **145**

A VERY SHORT LIST OF WHAT GREW IN THE UNITED STATES IN 1816 . . . . **148**

SOME QUESTIONS FOR THE READER, ALSO KNOWN AS YOU, PART IV . . . **151**

BANDITS AND BLUDGEONS **153**

WHEN YOU DON'T HAVE BREAD, WHO'S AFRAID OF PRISON? **155**

THESE GRUESOME FIGURES **160**

THE BRIGHT SUN WAS EXTINGUISH'D **163**

IT WAS ON A DREARY NIGHT **165**

A CASTLE ON A HILL **170**

WHAT THEY ATE **173**

A CONTINENT GROWLS WITH HUNGER **175**

PART III

THE DISTRESSING DIN **183**

THE WALKING DEAD **185**

SOME QUESTIONS FOR THE READER, ALSO KNOWN AS YOU, PART V **191**

SHOULD PEOPLE LIVE OR DIE? **195**

A SOUP OF THE DAY, EVERY DAY **197**

A WORLD IN MOTION **203**

UP AND OVER THE MOUNTAIN **205**

HOW TO MAKE A MAN INTO A HORSE **209**

THE VERY BEST OF INTENTIONS 215

    SHE WOULD NOT WASTE IT 217

    A FEVER DREAM 220

    SOME QUESTIONS FOR THE READER, ALSO KNOWN AS YOU, PART VI ...223

BELLS AND SINGING 227

    A WORLD EXHALES 229

NO ONE IMAGINED IT WAS MARY 235

    DANGEROUS WATERS 237

PART IV

THE TIME OF THE ASH RAIN 247

    YOU HAVE TO IMAGINE IT ABLAZE................................. 249

    A DISTORTION FIELD 252

    A QUESTION FOR THE READER, ALSO KNOWN AS YOU,
    AND THE AUTHOR, ALSO KNOWN AS ME................................ 256

    OUR CREATURE 258

    A DELICATE, DANGEROUS LINE 262

    A FINAL QUESTION FOR ALL OF US 265

ACKNOWLEDGMENTS...267

BIBLIOGRAPHY 269

NOTES 277

INDEX...291

IT WAS
A WARNING

The only way to understand is to have been there.

The word *loud* isn't loud enough. The word *hot* isn't hot enough. The word—

None of the words are enough.

The only way to understand is to have been there.

But if you had been there, you would be—

—well, you would be dead.

So we will do the best we can.

———◇———

This is a story about a volcano.

It's about the legendary eruption that destroyed the volcano. Before the eruption, this volcano was beautiful, its slopes green, its valleys rich. The island it sat on hummed with life. After the eruption, it was a shattered wreck, a literal shell of itself. It was gray, lifeless, an apocalyptic landscape of ash and bone.

And over the next few years, the fallout from that eruption would turn the whole world gray.

The weather would go haywire. It would bring famine, disease, death. No one living through it knew what was happening or why. No one knew if life would ever be the same.

It was a climate shock—a sudden, terrifying shift in the seasons.

All over the world, people discovered that the things they'd taken for granted were no longer to be taken for granted. They'd lived by the grace of a habitable planet. They'd lived by the grace of a habitable climate. Suddenly, all that was *gone*.

Then the skies shifted. The weather changed. The horrors vanished.

It was all forgotten—the chaos, the uncertainty, the fear. The fact that we live by the grace of a habitable planet, a habitable climate—that was forgotten, too.

But it shouldn't have been.

It was a warning.

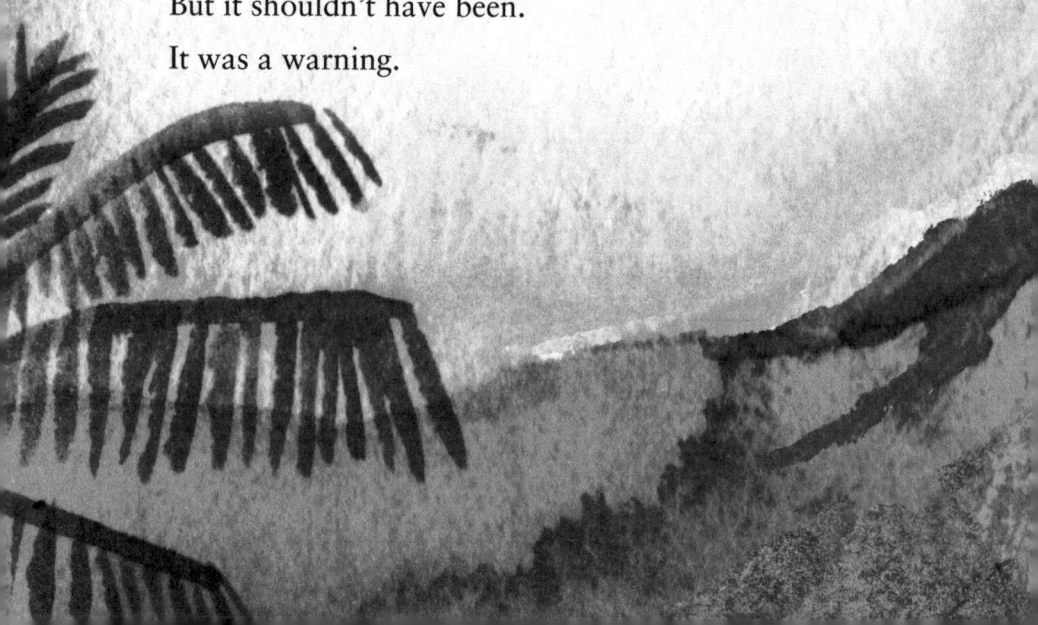

PART I

TECTONIC PLATES AND MOLTEN ROCK—KOMODO
DRAGONS—PEARL-DIVING AND HONEY-HARVESTING—
SLAVE TRADERS—COLONIAL OUTPOSTS—MYSTERIOUS
CANNONS—FOUNTAINS OF FLAME—BOILING
SEAS—FLOATING FORESTS—RIVERS OF FIRE—A
DAY TURNS TO NIGHT—A WORLD TURNS INSIDE
OUT—A LOST PEOPLE—A VEIL OF ASH AND ACID

FIRE AND FURY

MOUNT TAMBORA, INDONESIA
1815

THE GODS
WOULD RISE UP

This is how it starts.

Far beneath the earth's surface, a tectonic plate slips.

A tectonic plate is always slipping. That's what they do, slip. The earth is covered with these plates, and they slide around the crust, moving a tiny amount each year, a few inches at most. Each plate is in motion, and each grinds into the next, or pulls apart, or collides.

Down below, the pressure is tremendous. The temperature is preposterous. There is so much pressure and so much heat that fluid is pushed out of solid rock. These fluids rise, and as they rise they melt the rock above.

This molten rock is called magma, and it is threaded with gas and thick with minerals and water vapor. It is buoyed by the gas, and therefore lighter than the rock around it. It rises. It moves toward the surface, weaving its way through cracks and fissures in the crust.

It is still rising, melting more rock along the way, a balloon of melted rock and gas.

And then—usually—it stops. It stays. It cools.

But not always.

Because sometimes it keeps moving, shifting, rising.

Sometimes it finds a way out.

———◇———

On the morning of April 5, 1815, the *Benares* sat in port in Makassar, in what today we call Indonesia.

The *Benares* was a cruiser, a sailing ship from the East India Company, which effectively governed the British Empire in Asia. There was nothing special about the *Benares* itself. It was a trade ship among the many trade ships that sailed through these islands.

What was special about the *Benares* was the *where* and the *when*.

On April 5, 1815, it was several days of good sailing from the island of Sumbawa. This island was far from the larger Indonesian islands like Java, far from the larger cities like Batavia, now known as Jakarta. But on the shore of Sumbawa was an extraordinary sight: a single peak rising up before the morning sun on the horizon, the highest peak in a long trail of island peaks.

This was Tambora.

It was stunning, a dictionary-perfect definition of a volcano.

The *Benares* was headed in its direction.

Tambora would be gone before it got there.

———◇———

Indonesia is a chain of islands, an archipelago. It was made by volcanoes, and it will be remade by volcanoes. Today there are seventy-six active volcanoes, and hundreds more that are inactive. We have records of well over a thousand eruptions on the islands, and before records existed there were many thousands more.

This is because Indonesia sits at the intersection of massive tectonic plates: the Eurasian and the Australian. The Australian plate is moving faster—some eight centimeters a year, triple the speed of its partner—and it slips under the edge of the Eurasian plate.

Those few centimeters are the scene of tremendous, slow-moving violence. Sumbawa is tucked just off the edge of the Pacific Ocean, which is named for how it looks: *pacific,* or peaceful.

It is not.

Underneath the surface, far beneath, it is being ripped apart.

The archipelago was a land of unbelievable natural beauty.

Or at least it was unbelievable to the European colonists who'd arrived there a few centuries before. They were stunned by what they'd found. The land was saturated with life. Even the colors were more vivid than back home, the greens greener, the blues bluer.

To the native inhabitants, this was all very believable. It *was* home.

But the longtime residents of these islands were no longer alone. The islands—part of what was then known as the East Indies to Europeans—were scattered through the waters between Australia and Vietnam and the Philippines. Rich in spices and a perfect stopover on trade routes, the East Indies had long ago caught the eye of countries expanding their colonial holdings. The Dutch claimed the archipelago in the early 1600s, but the English had recently taken control, and they'd installed on the island of Java an official named Stamford Raffles. He would be the governor of the new colony. Raffles wanted to establish the islands as a cornerstone of the British Empire. They would supply Britain with coffee and sugar, he thought, and they would give the British Navy a perch from which to defend its colonies.

Raffles was an industrious man. He learned the local languages; he surveyed the terrain; he collected the indigenous plants and animals. But even though he wrote a history of Java, he saw it as a land *without* history—an idyllic, abundant land full of possibility. He wrote back home of the improbable fertility of the land: "The whole country, as seen from mountains of considerable elevation, appears a rich, diversified, and well watered garden." The fact that there were people who lived there already, people with their own rich cultures, people with their own history—that fact was glossed over.

Those people knew this land intimately. They knew that the agricultural dreams of the Dutch and the British—their sprawling new sugar plantations—were ruining this "rich, diversified, and well watered garden." The new European-made canals designed to irrigate the plantations were already stagnant. The sitting water attracted mosquitoes. Malaria was on the rise.

Raffles saw none of this: "The traveler can hardly advance five miles inland without feeling a sensible improvement in the atmosphere and climate. As he proceeds, at every step he breathes a purer air and surveys a brighter scene." Raffles was selling this paradise to his readers in Britain. But his very presence was ruining any paradise that he'd found.

The seas of Indonesia were deep, but British knowledge was shallow. Even the famous Komodo dragons of the nearby Komodo Island—massive creatures, the largest lizards in existence—were unknown to its occupiers. (They were not discovered by Europeans for another century.)

And Raffles did not know about the cataclysm that was about to tear apart these islands.

In the long volcanic history of the archipelago, the Europeans were a blip. But the people who were there long before the Europeans knew about the violence of the volcanoes. The eruptions were embedded in their stories and beliefs. The locals did not know when, but they knew it would happen.

It was inevitable: the gods below would rise up.

And the land would light itself on fire and split itself apart.

THE WORLD TURNED
TO BURNING ASH

SUMBAWA, APRIL 1815

The weather was warm; the rainfall was plentiful; the soil was rich. The crops ripened multiple times a year, and that April, the rice harvest was about to arrive. Thick forests climbed the sides of Tambora, which sat on a peninsula, towering over the island.

Sumbawa was small, but it was divided up among a half dozen princes, and it was a remarkably diverse place—the villagers on the far side of the island looked nothing like the villagers on the near side, and their languages were so different they were unable to understand each other. They logged sandalwood, or dove for pearls, or harvested honey, or raked the salt flats. They reared horses, too: the princes had been breeding horses for centuries, and the horse breeds of the island had become legendary. All these animals and goods could be traded, and traders of all sorts passed through Sumbawa.

But there were pirates, too.

And these pirates were after not just spoils, but people. There was a massive slave trade in the region. For centuries, the Dutch and the English had transported huge numbers of slaves through these waters. This colonial trafficking in slavery was now in very slow decline, but there were still pirates on the same mission, and they supplied the slave trade by sailing up in stealth and kidnapping whole villages before anyone could escape.

On a map, Sumbawa looked isolated. It was not. The chaos of the world had come to it: the colonial violence, the piratical plunder, the inhumanity of the slave trade.

Soon, however, the flow of influence would go the other way.

Soon, Sumbawa would bring chaos to the rest of the world.

———◊———

For many years, Tambora had been considered an extinct volcano. It had been quiet for generation after generation. It had slept for more than four hundred years.

Until a few weeks before that April, at least, when it began to rumble. It even belched out ash. The Sumbawans had theories for why. The noise was celebratory—there'd been a marriage among the gods, and the rumbling was the reception for this divine wedding. Or—and this theory was more troubling—the turmoil was a sign of divine anger. The gods were enraged that the Europeans—first the Dutch, now the British—had taken over the islands, destroying local traditions and forcing many to work on plantations.

The Sumbawans were right to suspect trouble.

Because deep inside Tambora, the magma had begun to rise.

It was looking for a way out.

———◇———

It was Wednesday—April 5, 1815—when the commander of the *Benares* heard the sound of the East Indies being attacked. The battle was not visible, but the noise was unmistakable. It was cannons echoing across the waters.

"Heavy guns," he noted. The battle seemed serious. Each report of cannon fire sounded as if it drew nearer. It lasted all afternoon. The *Benares* was moored, and the commander ordered the ship put to sea. It spent all that day, and the next, and the next, searching for the sounds.

But the search turned up nothing. There were no pirates, no slave traders, no rogue Dutch vessels. There were no cannons.

From the island of Java, some eight hundred miles away, Stamford Raffles also heard what sounded like cannons. Troops were dispatched to "a neighboring post" that was under attack. Vessels were sent to help a "ship in distress." British officials worried that villages far inside the islands had gone to war against their colonial rule.

The "neighboring post" was not under attack. The "ship in distress" was not there. The villages were at peace.

It was all extremely confusing.

The cannons did not go silent. They roared throughout the night, and no matter where someone was, it seemed as if the echoes came from close by. They were too loud, too thunderous, to be far away.

Not everyone heard cannons, though.

The priests on Java—the same island where Stamford Raffles sat—heard something very different than the British official did.

They heard the anger and power of their gods.

———◇———

That same Wednesday, the people closest to Tambora were not confused.

They did not go looking for cannons. They did not go looking for ships.

They looked up.

Thousands of feet above, Tambora was on fire. Out of its peak came a fountain of flame. Its slopes shook like they were splitting apart. And the sound—it was so loud it must have been more like a feeling, more like a state, than a sound.

Among the first to hear it was the raja of Sanggar, who ruled over the territory on the slopes of Tambora, as close to the volcano as any part of the island. It was a beautiful sweep of land, gently rolling down into the sea.

It was now the scene of a nightmare.

As darkness fell, the flames grew brighter. The noise was unrelenting. Clouds of ash fell through the flames and blanketed the rice paddies, which trembled, shaking along with everyone and everything else.

And then it stopped. Ash still drifted down, and Tambora still rumbled, but the nightmare had ended. Even the rice harvest could be saved, if the ash was cleaned off the paddies.

To the raja, who knew how violent volcanoes could be, it must have felt like a narrow escape.

———◇———

In the days after the nightmare, the raja sent his people to sweep ash off the rice.

On April 6, they toiled.

On April 7, they toiled.

On April 8, and 9, and 10, they toiled.

On April 11, they did not.

———◇———

On the evening of April 10—as hopes rose that the volcano had fallen back asleep—Tambora blew itself apart.

This time, there were many columns of fire, shooting far higher than before, and this time, the fire came down the mountain. Pouring out of the peak, the lava raced down the slopes. It burned and buried all it passed over, reaching speeds of nearly twenty miles an hour.

It was as if the earth had been turned inside out and its glowing center was now on the *outside*.

Then the rain came, but in this inside-out world, it was not rain but rock. The magma that was shot from the summit instantly cooled into pumice, a lightweight, porous volcanic rock. It fell in massive, deadly showers through air that was clogged with dust. Eventually, the air was so thick it obscured even the columns of fire.

In a dense cloud of ash, everything vanishes. There is no sun. There is no noon, no night. There is no sky, no stars.

There is nothing.

In the dark, the mountain was now exploding in every direction.

To understand what happened next, we need to talk through the words *pyroclastic flow*. It is the sort of term that hides its horror.

Pyro is for fire.

Clastic is for broken pieces of rock.

Pyroclastic flow: a river of burning rock, or magma.

It sounds bad. It gets worse.

In a pyroclastic flow, the magma flows on a current of toxic gases, heated beyond 1,000 degrees Fahrenheit. This is a temperature so hot it can melt glass, and the flow moves faster than a getaway car, racing down a volcano at speeds well above one hundred miles an hour. Hot air normally rises. But a pyroclastic flow is *heavy*, because it is part rock—the rock that moments before was the volcano itself. A pyroclastic flow has a mountain suspended inside it.

A volcanologist once sought a way to describe the horror of a pyroclastic flow. It combines, he wrote, "the qualities of an atomic bomb blast, an immense avalanche, and a Category Five hurricane." Plus, the volcanologist added, almost as an after-thought, there is "the added complication" of the temperatures.

No one caught in a pyroclastic flow survives. It kills instantly.

In the worst volcanic disaster of the twentieth century, the quiet island of Martinique exploded with the eruption of Mount Pelée. The eruption was survivable. The pyroclastic flow was not. It barreled into the small town of Saint-Pierre at the base of the volcano. Saint-Pierre had a population of 28,000 people.

There were *two* survivors.

One was on the edge of the city. One was in a dungeon.

It was this demonic phenomenon that now sped down the slopes of Tambora.

The heavy layer of superheated air and gas and rock smoth-ered the land. When that unbelievably hot air finally rose, it rose so quickly that it left nothing where it had been—for a very brief moment, that space in the atmosphere was essentially empty. New air rushed in to fill the void, and it filled it with a suddenness and violence that created whirlwinds. The force was so powerful it sent houses and trees flying into the air. Whole villages were torn up by the roots. Many landed in the sea, which was steaming from the rivers of lava running into it.

In this upside-down world, the sea was boiling.

Under the water, there was no escape. The pyroclastic flow coated the seafloor. It killed all ocean life for miles.

Wherever the pyroclastic flows hit the cold water, they triggered a series of secondary eruptions. These eruptions sent even more ash and steam into the air. There were now explosions erupting upward from Tambora itself *and* from the edges of the island.

The island was trapped in a cloud of steam and ash, rock and gas.

The resulting scene was unfathomable.

The villages surrounding the volcano were crushed, inciner-ated, torn up, torn down, buried. They lay beneath deposits of ash and pumice that were deeper than any person is tall. The residents of the villages closest were simply petrified. They were turned into charcoal.

There was almost no way out, and yet the raja escaped. The only way to survive was to leave immediately, and leave at speed, and apparently the raja and his family did, presumably on the horses for which the island was famous. There was a narrow window of time and an even narrower path to safety, and somehow the raja found it.

His is the only eyewitness account of the eruption from Tambora, and we have but a summary recorded months later by a British representative: "The whole mountain appeared like a body of liquid fire, extending itself in every direc-tion." The flames raged "with unabated fury" until the ash was so thick that it "obscured" them. Then the stones, "as large as two fists"; then the "violent whirlwind, which blew down every house in the village"; then the sea, "sweeping away houses and everything within its reach. . . . There were certainly not fewer than twelve thousand individuals in [the immediate area] at the time of the eruption, of whom only five or six survive."

What do we say about those people—the people who van-ished in Tambora's ashes?

Their story is lost. It has vanished, too.

We can say that many of those closest to Tambora—perhaps almost all—perished. But that does not do their story justice. This is where fiction sometimes sneaks in: we want to fill in the gaps, we want to exercise our imaginations. The bare facts we have are so *bare*. They are not enough.

But this is a book about what we know, and only what we know. There is no imagination here. So our story must lean on the written records.

Because the voices of Tambora itself are silent.

———◇———

When Tambora erupted, the crew of the *Benares*—the ship from the East India Company, moored hundreds of miles from the volcano—were still hearing what they thought were cannons: "The firing was again heard but much louder, and towards morning the reports were in quick succession, and sometimes like three or four guns fired together, and so heavy that they shook the ships, as they did the houses in the fort."

Then the skies grew darker, then redder, then darker still. And then from the skies, a sort of storm gathered and it began to rain—a fine layer of volcanic ash.

It was only then, when the first flakes fell on deck, that the sailors on the *Benares* knew what had happened.

The skies opened up. They poured ash. "The darkness was so profound throughout the remainder of the day that I never saw any thing equal to it in the darkest night," wrote the commander of the *Benares*. "It was impossible to see your hand when held up close to the eye."

The ash fell by day. It fell by night. When the ship could be seen again, it looked as if it had been petrified: the heavy ash—a fine powder of rocks and minerals—lay over everything in "heaps" a foot deep. It was as if the ship itself had turned into a gigantic pumice stone.

The *Benares* was now trying to make its way through these waters. Unfortunately, its route took it *closer* to the eruption—and as it approached, the crew found the sea almost impassable.

The sea was clogged with *land*.

There was a dry sandbank where no sandbank should be. The ship grew closer. This was no sandbank. It was a field of rocks, as far as the eye could see. Pumice is a sort of geologic magic trick: lava, or molten rock, is frothed up with volcanic gas; when the rock cools, the gas bubbles are trapped—and the rock is part air. It is so light it floats.

The pumice in the seas around Tambora was as deep as fifteen feet.

The *Benares* sailed through rock, an impossible feat. On top of the rock lay whole trees, black and "burnt," as if "blasted by lightning." It was an alien landscape. "The sea was literally covered with shoals of pumice and floating timber."

The forests of Sumbawa had been extensive. They now extended into the sea.

After all this—after the columns of fire, the hail of rocks, the clouds of toxic gas, the full-dress rehearsal for the apocalypse—after all this, Tambora fell.

It had nothing left to hold it up, and so it collapsed. Tambora was now a shrunken giant. Its top third was missing, some five thousand feet of volcano just *gone*. What remained was a caldera, or a sort of hollow bowl. It was massive, measuring thousands of feet down and miles wide. It ranks among the largest caldera created since the last ice age.

That bowl had been filled with Tambora itself.

But Tambora was now in the air—a towering, billowing column of gray.

———◇———

The numbers are numbing.

The plume from the eruption reached a staggering *twenty-seven miles* high.

Past Mount Everest, past the highest clouds, past the ozone layer, up where the air is too thin to breathe and too cold to bear. Up where only rockets go. It would take over a century of physics and engineering to get anything that high again.

The sound was heard over sixteen hundred miles away—it was as if a door slammed in Florida and was heard in Maine. "The sound appeared to be so close," an observer noted, "that in each district it seemed near at hand." On the opposite side of Sumbawa, some forty miles away from Tambora, a British official said the eruption was like "a heavy mortar fired close to his ear."

We have estimates today of how much Tambora sent skyward.

Imagine a square with sides a hundred miles long. Now fence it in: make the sides a dozen feet high. Everything inside that space could be filled to the brim with what used to be Tambora.

There is a scale called the Volcanic Explosivity Index, or VEI. It takes the immense complexity of a volcanic eruption—the quantity, the height, that sort of thing—and reduces it all to a number. The scale runs from 0 to 8, and it is logarithmic. That means that each number represents an eruption ten *times* more powerful than the number before.

The eruption in AD 79 of Mount Vesuvius in Italy—the volcano that buried the Roman town of Pompeii—is a 5. The legendary 1883 Krakatoa eruption is a 6. Because the Volcanic Explosivity Index is logarithmic, the Krakatoa eruption is therefore ten times stronger than the eruption of Vesuvius.

The eruption of Tambora is a 7. It is a hundred times stronger than Vesuvius, ten times stronger than Krakatoa.

Well over three thousand years ago, the extraordinary Minoan eruption shattered the Greek island of Crete. It was an eruption so powerful it utterly destroyed what is often called the first advanced civilization in Europe.

Tambora was more powerful than *that*.

It is the most powerful eruption since the last ice age.

———◇———

In the aftermath of the eruption, the sun suffered a sort of volcanic eclipse.

Across the islands, it went out.

There was only light enough to see the ash—the dust, the constant dust—as it piled up everywhere. There were days of this darkness. When the sun finally appeared again, it was dim, more like a reminder of the sun than the sun itself.

The birds of the islands were so spooked they fell silent.

For a week, all of Southeast Asia lay under the shadow of Tambora.

In the darkness, the waves came. A tsunami triggered by the eruption swept across the islands. A wall of water some twelve feet high raced up onto the shores. Houses and boats were uprooted and thrown on top of each other.

First, the land had risen up. Now the ocean was rising up, too.

On Sumbawa, there were survivors lucky enough to be farther from the volcano, but unlucky enough to be on the same island. They soon discovered there was nothing on the island to eat. There was nothing to drink, either. The ash soaked into the water. Swallowing dissolved ash causes severe diarrhea, which can lead to dehydration and death. Those who avoided that fate still breathed in air that was thick with ash. They began to cough, and they never stopped. It was a horrible spiral.

The dead of the island had long been buried with precious possessions to aid them in the afterlife. Now villagers dug up those precious possessions. They needed them to barter for food.

But what food?

Horses, once the prize of Sumbawa, were eaten, and soon, there were no horses.

There was nothing but coconuts, and soon, there were no coconuts.

Soon, those who had dug up the dead would be dead, too.

No one was safe. The raja's own daughter died of starvation.

The winds blew the ash west, where it fell so heavily that it collapsed roofs across the islands. It brought the same nightmarish problems: disease, famine, death.

———◇———

And then—

How do we tell this part?

It feels beyond telling.

When Stamford Raffles first arrived in the islands as the British official in charge—several years before Tambora erupted—he abolished slave trading. He shut down the open-air slave markets. This did not get rid of slavery—there were too many islands and there were too many slave traders, too many pirates. But it made it markedly more difficult.

In the chaotic, desperate days after the eruption, this decision would have unforeseen consequences. Because in this bizarre world—an upside-down world, a world in which the sea boiled—in this world, people *wanted* to be sold.

It was a logical decision. They had no food, no water. They had no hope. Liberty mattered less than life. Slavery, even into servitude that would last a lifetime, looked better than death. Parents went to the shores, hoping to sell their children.

They died there, waiting to be saved. Waiting to be saved by *slave traders*.

Slave traders who never came.

It is an incredible scene to imagine—impossible, really—but that is the point.

The world that Tambora made stretches far beyond our humble imaginations.

———◇———

In August, months after the eruption, the scale of the devastation finally dawned on Stamford Raffles.

He sent a ship with a few hundred tons of rice toward Sumbawa. It was enough to feed twenty thousand people for a week, the people who'd been lucky enough to be farthest from Tambora. It was not enough. It was not nearly enough.

Lieutenant Owen Philipps, who'd been sent along to investigate, grimly surveyed the land. There were no trees. There were no plants.

Around Tambora, there were no *people*.

The princedom of Tambora itself was completely destroyed. Its language was gone—it would never be heard again.

———◇———

A decade after Tambora erupted, a poet from Bima, on the other side of Sumbawa, wrote:

The mountain reverberated around us
As torrents of water mixed with ash fell from the sky.
Children screamed and wept, and their mothers, too,
Believing the world had been turned to burning ash.

———◇———

Over one hundred thousand people were killed more or less directly by Tambora.

This number is likely an underestimate. The true toll may be twice that, easily. In the months and years after Tambora, disease and famine spread to the surrounding islands, including far more populated ones.

The eruption of Tambora is the most deadly eruption in history.

And these were only the *direct* deaths—the people who lived on or around Tambora. These people knew why they were dying. They'd heard the eruption. They'd seen the fire. They'd felt the ash.

The people who would die later—years later—had no idea they were victims of Tambora, too.

A NATURAL EXPERIMENT

The thick ash from Tambora fell from the sky in the weeks after the eruption.

And then the sun—the sun that had been hidden behind all that ash—came out.

It was a mixed blessing. Because when the sun came out, it lit up a landscape of horror. The birds were gone, the bees were gone. The horses were gone. The people were gone.

Tambora was still there, jagged, cut almost in half. It still rumbled. It wouldn't stop rumbling for years.

Five years later, the seas surrounding the volcano were still full of floating rocks. The land itself was still blackened.

Five years after that, the island was described as "a desolate heap of rubble."

Five years after *that,* it was described as "a horrendous scene of devastation." The eruption had spared "of the inhabitants, not a single person, of the fauna, not a worm, of the flora, not a blade of grass."

It was a sensational, ghastly scene, a sort of war zone without the war.

But few who had not seen or heard the eruption would ever know about Tambora.

The world was still large then. There was no radio, there were no telephones. There were no telegraphs, even. Reports of the eruption were carried by hand, or horse, or boat. They took up a few paragraphs in a few newspapers, and that was it. Tambora's monumental scale was never really known outside the region that it decimated.

The world was so large that a volcano could erupt with a force not known for more than a thousand years—and no one who wasn't there to see or hear it would notice.

And this is where our story would stop: an immense local tragedy, a singular natural disaster, a global footnote.

But it doesn't stop here.

Because the rest of the world *would* notice.

They just wouldn't know it was Tambora they were noticing.

———◇———

It all comes back to the ash.

Because not all of it fell. Only the coarse ash fell, the part people could see. The heaviest, thickest particles—those were dragged down by gravity.

But the finest particles were still there.

And they were heading straight up.

Rising alongside those fine particles was gas, a lot of it. These were the gases that were once dissolved in the magma; they'd powered the eruption. There were some fifty-five million tons of sulfur dioxide, and far above Tambora it combined with water vapor to make a compound called sulfuric acid. Each droplet of sulfuric acid is infinitesimally small. Gravity has little grasp on it, so it can float on the high, thin air of the stratosphere, many miles up.

Each individual droplet is meaningless. But Tambora produced massive quantities of these aerosols, fine droplets suspended in the air. Together they formed a veil that draped across the top of the sky. This veil—a mixture of sulfuric acid, ash, and dust—was of a staggering size: one hundred million tons.

Ash and aerosols can be washed out of the sky. But this layer was far above any rain cloud. Some of the sky is above the weather, and that part is the stratosphere, a region as dry as any desert.

In the years to come, this veil would float along the top of the stratosphere, moving with the currents of the air. It cursed the normal rhythms of the climate. It cursed the normal cycles of rain and sun.

No one knew the veil was there.

They just knew that something was *wrong*.

They were trapped in a natural experiment, an experiment that asked a very simple question:

What happens when the climate changes?

SOME QUESTIONS FOR THE READER, ALSO KNOWN AS YOU, PART I

How do you tell a story when the people in the story don't know what's happening?

How do you tell a story when the people in the story don't even know they're *in* a story?

It might seem a little strange to start asking you questions here.

But it seems only fair that you should be involved.

———◆———

Everyone near Tambora knew very well what was happening. They knew all too well.

But the weirdness of Tambora is that as we follow its story, as that story radiates outward, we lose the fact of Tambora. We are left with the consequences of Tambora, but not Tambora itself.

As this story leaves Indonesia, as it moves across the world, few people will know that a volcano erupted. Fewer people will know which volcano, and even fewer will know where. None will know why it matters. They won't know that their world is changing because of it. They will be stuck in a story that they can't comprehend. They will be stuck in a story they don't even know they're in.

Stories about the past are usually locked in time and place—something happened *there* and it happened *then*. The story of Tambora isn't like that.

It went global. It connected everyone, whether they knew it or not.

———◇———

It isn't locked in time, either.

The fallout from Tambora will land in the present—our today and our tomorrow.

We regret to say that this is your story, too. You're just like everyone else here: you're stuck in a story you didn't even know you were in.

So it seems only fair to involve you.

PART II

A FEVER—A COMET—DISOBEDIENCE—TIME TRAVEL—
DOWNPOURS AND DIVINE DISPLEASURE—GLUTTONY—
SCANDAL—SNOW IN MAY—GOBLETS OF GOLD—THE
END OF THE WORLD—EIGHT ENORMOUS DOGS AND
THREE MONKEYS—RIOTS—A GHOST STORY—SNOW
IN JUNE—FIRE AND BANDITS—A RHINOCEROS—A
NIGHTMARE—AN AVALANCHE—DARKNESS—SNAILS—
SNOW IN JULY—A CASTLE—BOILED GRASS—A
SPOTTED SUN—ICELAND—FAMINE—A SILENT NIGHT

A DEATH
AND A BIRTH

LONDON
1797 AND 1815

A COMET IN THE SKY

While Tambora exploded, Mary Godwin read.

She read Voltaire, the French philosopher. It was before breakfast. Mary Godwin was the sort of teenager who read philosophy before breakfast.

She was in London. She had no idea that Tambora had erupted.

She was a writer, not a wizard. She couldn't see what was happening on the far side of the globe.

She couldn't see into the future, either.

She couldn't see that Tambora would change her life.

———◇———

Disaster is local.

At least that's what we expect.

We expect that if an earthquake levels Japan, everyone in Italy will be fine. If a tornado tears through Kansas, no one in

Maine will be affected. And we assume that if a volcano flattens an island in Indonesia, life in the high Swiss mountain valleys will go on just as it did before. The cows there will keep grazing.

So when we read in the news that a tsunami has wiped out a coastal island, we feel many things: heartbroken, distressed, sorrowful.

But we don't feel *scared.*

The eruption of Tambora doesn't follow this pattern.

The event is local, but the effects are global. It's as if there were a tsunami and everyone everywhere got swept away.

Those Swiss mountain valleys—to pick a point on the globe—are as far from Tambora as it is possible to get. But the cows there are not safe. They do not keep grazing.

Mary Godwin was far from Tambora, almost as far as anyone could be. She likely never knew that it had erupted. But its reverberations would shake her world, and they would inspire her to write a story, and that story would become legendary.

The history of Tambora includes many stories of suffering. But there are also stories of invention and genius. Stories that wouldn't exist without Tambora. And the most extraordinary of these is a story *about* a story.

A story sparked by the terrifying weather of Tambora. A story that speaks to our own terrifying weather today.

Terror shadowed Mary Godwin—soon to be Mary Shelley— her whole life.

It began with her birth.

LONDON, 1797

She wouldn't live. It was clear as soon as the baby was born. Sick, small, closer to death than to life. There was nothing to do but swaddle her.

The more urgent matter was saving the mother.

The woman in the bed was Mary Wollstonecraft, a brilliant, fearless philosopher who'd dared to argue that women were in no way inferior to men. Famously spirited, she was now weak. Her body was worn out, and it would not deliver the afterbirth, the placenta. A doctor was called in. He found the placenta and cut it out. Then he left.

He'd killed Mary Wollstonecraft.

She was still alive for now, but he'd killed her.

The doctor hadn't washed his hands—no doctors did then; no one understood how germs worked—and so when he'd taken out the placenta, he'd introduced disease. It was a disease that afflicted women who'd given birth, a disease known as puerperal fever.

It took Mary Wollstonecraft ten agonizing days to die.

This was a woman who'd written piercingly on the unfairness of the lives of women, the oppression and injustice they faced. And now she faced the death of so many women before her, a death that no man would ever face.

Mary Wollstonecraft, so powerful, would die.

But her child, so small and sickly, would live.

That child would become Mary Godwin, and then Mary Shelley, and she would not stay sick for long.

She would become brilliant and fearless, like the mother she'd just left.

The month she was born, a comet split apart the London sky.

———◇———

Mary Godwin grew up in the house where she'd been born. It was where her mother had died, in a small bedroom on an upper landing. The room was nothing special, unless you knew what had happened there, unless you were Mary, and then it must have been everything.

But her house was not a place of mourning. It was an extraordinarily lively place, and it was lit with intellectual firepower. All the luminaries of the era passed through her household: the revolutionary Thomas Paine, the visionary William Blake, the poet William Wordsworth.

They were there for William Godwin, Mary's father, a radical publisher and philosopher. And Mary was there because Godwin dared to take his daughter seriously. This was unusual. Children, especially girls, were not taken seriously at the time. They might become interesting, but they certainly weren't as children. Godwin believed none of this. He believed in a spirited, intellectually rich home, in which Mary and her sister Jane—the daughter of Godwin's new wife—were always included. Mary and Jane were hiding behind the sofa when the great poet Samuel Taylor Coleridge read his extraordinary work, *The Rime of the Ancient Mariner*. They were discovered. They were allowed to stay.

Mary was always allowed to stay. The world turned toward her. Some people saw her beauty first. Her hair was reddish, a sort of strawberry blond, and her features delicate. Her eyes were large, and they seemed to take in everything and everyone.

Some people saw her genius first.

Godwin cultivated that genius. The world was wondrous, but knowing about its wonders was not enough, he thought. The world was complex and you had to work your way through those complexities. You had to know how to *reason*.

Children were taught to obey, but Godwin thought obedience was poor training. Since the world is wondrous and complex, you will never know everything the world demands. You won't know *what* to obey. You won't know when to be disobedient.

Godwin observed his daughter. She was, he wrote, "singularly bold, somewhat imperious and active of mind, her desire of knowledge is great, and her perseverance in everything she undertakes, almost invincible."

She was, in other words, an extremely good student.

She was a good student in a different way, too.

She'd learned the deeper lessons her father taught had her: how to reason, how to think for herself.

How to disobey.

And Mary would grow up to be extremely disobedient.

The year after Tambora, Mary would arrive in a country where she wasn't supposed to be, with a man she wasn't supposed to be with, with a child she wasn't supposed to have.

She would be just eighteen.

The sky would go wild above her. It would be a Tambora sky—half a world away from Tambora, but very much the same world, the same Earth.

Under those volcanic bolts of lightning, Mary would pick up her pen.

And she would bring a horrifying creature to life.

It haunts us still.

RED SKIES AND RED SNOW

ENGLAND
EUROPE
THE STRATOSPHERE
WINTER 1815 AND SPRING 1816

A FEEDBACK LOOP OF BAD

Only a month after Tambora erupted, its veil of ash and acid, now high in the stratosphere, had circled the equator.

It would not stay there.

The atmosphere does not stand still. The sun strikes it at different angles at different times and warms what's below at different speeds. Nothing about this system is simple. What matters is that it is profoundly *uneven*. This unevenness is what generates movement in the atmosphere. Warm air continually rises; cold air continually rushes in. There's turbulence. There's motion. This is why we have wind. This is why we have weather.

This is why Tambora did not stick around Tambora.

All that movement took what was once Tambora and pulled it from pole to pole.

Within a few months, it shadowed the globe.

By the end of June, a few months after Tambora erupted, glorious sunsets were recorded in London.

These were twilight skies of transcendent color, and they stayed lit long after the sun went down, orange and red at the horizon and purple and pink high overhead. They were streaked with mysterious dark bands, and they lingered in the sky.

We see red skies at dawn and dusk because that's when sunlight has to travel through more of the atmosphere to reach us. This journey through the atmosphere scatters the blue end of the light spectrum—the shorter wavelengths. The red end—the longer wavelengths—survive. That's why our sunsets and sunrises are red and not blue.

In the aftermath of a volcano, a sunset has to pass through a haze of dust and sulfur dioxide, too. These also scatter the blue and preserve the red. An already red sunset gets *redder*. It's as if the volume on the sunset is turned all the way up.

This is why the skies above England were skies of fire. They were a ghostly mirror of what the people of Tambora saw above them.

We can still see these sunsets today, caught by the brush of J. M. W. Turner, the English painter. Turner paid such close attention to the sky that he kept a sketchbook of it. In his watercolors, we can see the work of Tambora far above in the stratosphere, scattering the light spectrum into vibrant bands.

In London, to look at the sunset was to see the volcano still glowing.

It was beautiful, as long as you couldn't see the horror behind the beauty.

No one could.

No one beholding this beauty knew they were seeing Tambora.

No one in London even knew Tambora had erupted.

The few people outside Indonesia who did know about Tambora had no inkling that the eruption would affect places far from Asia. It was a volcano on the other side of the world from Europe. Why would it affect anything there? How could it?

It would have made no sense.

At the time of Tambora, no one knew how volcanoes worked.

But no one knew how the weather worked, either, not yet.

That would soon change.

———◆———

There was more than Tambora in those sunsets.

We know this today because we have a record of the atmosphere of the Tambora years. It's a record that's written in ice. When snowflakes fall, they trap air and dust and whatever else happens to be in the atmosphere. More snow falls on top of that snow, and the weight of each snowfall compacts the snowfall before it. The layers of snow on the ground get thinner and denser, and in Antarctica or Greenland, those layers never melt. With each year, they get even thinner, even denser. They turn into ice.

Trapped in this ice are the air and the dust and whatever else happened to be in the atmosphere. There are bubbles, too—microscopic bubbles, squeezed into flat discs. Inside each bubble is the chemical signature of the atmosphere at that precise moment.

To read this history, scientists drill straight down and extract a long, thin rod of ice. This is called an ice core, but it could be called a time machine. Fifty feet down is the equivalent of two hundred years back in time. Scientists have gone almost two miles down. They have gone almost a million years back in time.

Inside each ice core is a detailed record of the climate. It tells the temperature. It tells the pollution levels. It tells how much pollen was floating through the air, how much sunlight was reflecting off the snow, which direction the wind was blowing.

And it tells us about volcanoes on the far side of the world.

A major eruption leaves a stripe of brown ash across the ice core. It practically shouts:

A volcano exploded!

You can see Tambora in these cores of ice.

You can see Mayon, a volcano in the Philippines that erupted the year before Tambora.

And you can see, a half decade before that, something else.

An absolutely massive something else.

In the year 1809, a volcano erupted *somewhere.* It was the second-largest eruption of the past five hundred years. The only larger eruption was Tambora.

This 1809 volcano—we have no idea what it was or even *where* it was. It's a total mystery. Without the ice, we would never have known about it at all. It was an extraordinary eruption that vanished with only a trace.

A trace found hundreds of feet below Greenland.

This means that Tambora was the final eruption in a string of eruptions. Before Tambora, there was already a fine mist of aerosols and ash in the atmosphere. The climate of the earth had already been jolted. It was already wobbling. Accounts from the period are a litany of disappointment: this winter was *little better;* this spring was *little better;* this summer was *little better.*

The volcanic weather was already there, before Tambora had even erupted.

When Tambora did erupt, sending itself into the stratosphere, it sent a wobbly climate into a feedback loop.

The next year would not be *little better.*

The next year would be *very bad.*

IT WAS A SIGN

In Europe, the years were already bad enough.

For several decades before Tambora, the continent had been at war, the victim of a bloody brawl between the French emperor Napoléon Bonaparte and much of the rest of Europe. These Napoleonic wars had torn many countries to shreds. Villages were plundered; farms were stripped of their crops, even their seeds. Soldiers fell in bewildering numbers. When Napoléon invaded Russia in 1812, he headed an army of almost seven hundred thousand. On his pitiful, desperate retreat, he was accompanied by fewer than seventy thousand.

But by the end of 1815, treaties were signed. Napoléon had lost. He was exiled to a remote volcanic island halfway between South America and Africa. (It did not erupt.) The fighting was over.

A continent exhaled. Finally, this coming year—1816—would be a good year.

Yes, the last year had been a bad year, and the year before that, too. The whole decade had been bad, in fact, and the decade before. But that was over. The wars were over. The armies were going home. In the future, there would be peace, and there would be milk and honey.

The newspapers and magazines welcomed this promising year with poetry and optimism. A German poet concluded his hymn to the new year with the lines:

From heaven today I wish for you
The finest sunshine, which ensures
That the wheat will ripen unsoaked
In the great barn of peoples.

No part of his wish would be granted.

———◇———

The first sign of trouble in the skies arrived with the snow that December in Italy, just over a half year after Tambora erupted.

It was December, so the snow was not a surprise, not really. The amount was a surprise. It was "the heaviest snow ever known in that country." But the heaviest snow of all time in central Italy had to fall *sometime*. It might as well be December 1815.

The amount was not why the snow had "excited great fear and apprehension in the people." It was not why the town held religious ceremonies to soothe the feelings of an upset God.

That was because of the color.

The snow was not white.

It was red, or yellow, or sometimes red *and* yellow.

A few weeks after the Italian blizzard, it snowed in Hungary. This snow was not red or yellow.

It was brown, a brown blizzard, burying houses and cattle under brown snow.

The towering clouds behind these blizzards in Italy and Hungary had slipped into the stratosphere, where ash from Tambora stained the ice crystals that fell as snow. This happened infrequently—storm clouds rarely stray into the stratosphere. But when it did, the results were hair-raising.

The snow was Tambora's signature. It was a sign, a forewarning of the year to come, and that sign said: *What on earth is going on here?*

———◇———

Luke Howard looked up at the sky. This wasn't unusual. Luke Howard was always looking up.

An English chemist, Howard was an unlikely celebrity for an unlikely reason: he was the man who'd named the clouds.

Not names like Henry or Estella. Names like *stratus* and *cumulus*. A decade before Tambora, Howard had proposed a system for the identification and classification of clouds, his

Essay on the Modification of Clouds. It was a dry, detailed work, but in this period of astonishingly bad weather, it became a sort of sensation.

Weather is small talk when there is nothing else to say, but in this decade the weather *was* what there was to say. Even before Tambora, it was the obvious topic. Already under the veil of the earlier eruptions—the eruptions we can see in the ice core today—England was perpetually, exasperatingly cloudy (even by English standards).

To compensate for the lack of sun, English poets became bewitched by clouds. So did painters. John Constable—perhaps the greatest landscape painter of his time—got so into clouds that sometimes he painted *only* clouds. Even when he painted the rest of the landscape, the clouds often dominated the scene.

In the autumn of 1816, Constable was on his honeymoon in Weymouth Bay. It was a good place for a honeymoon, a famously warm beach on the famously cold English coast. But the painting that Constable made there is dark and dreary. In the painting, the winds blow fiercely. The sun is long gone. A couple at the edge of the beach—a couple that could be Constable himself and his bride—look as if they are about to be sacrificed to the storm.

There was no sun in England, even on the beach, even on your honeymoon.

Luke Howard saw all this. He'd been looking at the sky all his life, and even he had never seen the like before. Day after day, week after week, month after month, Luke Howard documented the daily toll of the new weird weather. Not a week into 1816, Howard noted "violent storms of wind and rain" throughout England. These were not occasional reports. They were daily. The severity of the storms was "beyond example."

These were storms of Tambora. Its eruption had rapidly cooled the air temperatures, but the land and the oceans, which store heat longer, had taken more time to lose their warmth. Now, a half year later, these elements were adjusting to their new reality. The still-warm oceans were throwing too much moisture into the air, and that moisture took shape as clouds, and those clouds took shape as storms. The normal currents—the jet streams, the well-worn patterns of air circulation—were suddenly out of whack, moving into unfamiliar territory, wreaking havoc.

The climate system of our planet has a sort of inertia. It is sluggish. But once it does change, it is very hard to change *back*.

For the climate, this new reality was, effectively, a new Earth.

———◇———

Luke Howard did not know any of this because when Tambora erupted, meteorology—the study of weather—was "in its earliest infancy."

In 1816, the tools to understand the world were not scientific but biblical. Early scientists were often ministers and clergymen, and they aimed to make their discoveries fit within a biblical framework. Bad weather was understood morally: it was a sign of sin, of divine displeasure.

It was punishment.

It wasn't so much that people chose to interpret it this way. There was no other way to interpret it. This was the only framework, the only vocabulary. And if the weather was divinely ordained, there wasn't any reason to study it.

The most fundamental aspects of the climate were not understood. (Even the water cycle—the process by which water evaporates and condenses—had still not been explained.) There was no theory to account for how the climate worked—and even if someone had come up with a theory, it couldn't have been tested: there was too little data, and even that data wasn't any good.

Today we know that weather data is useful for making predictions. But no one then was trying to predict the weather, because the whole idea wouldn't have made any sense.

Predicting the weather was the same thing as predicting the *future*. It was not the work of science. It was the work of witches and wizards. It was supernatural. It was possibly even evil.

Tambora would change all that.

THUNDER ROLLED
DOWN THE YEAR

All that volcanic winter—the winter of the red and brown blizzards—the snow piled up across Great Britain. When it melted, the flooding was immense. The waters were "washing down bridges, overflowing the banks of rivers, and carrying away cattle." By February, even families once "prosperous" were "reduced to the lowest state of poverty." The fields were soaked through.

Thunder rolled. It would roll down the whole length of that year.

A pattern emerged. After days of rain, a respite would arrive—but not sun, never sun, just *not* rain. People would rejoice; God would be praised. But a cold snap would follow, and then rain, rain again. The hay, barely sprouted, spoiled in the fields. Boats floated in the streets.

"Never," wrote an Englishman in his diary, "or at least within memory of man, was such a time for general distress of the Nation."

———◇———

Meanwhile, the prince regent of England ate.

The prince effectively ruled England. His father, George III, suffered from an acute illness and had been stripped of his powers. But the prince took his duties less seriously than his hobbies. These were eating and gambling and drinking, although not in that order, because there was never an order. The prince wanted all his pleasures at once. His appetite was prodigious and shocked those who saw him at the table. At breakfast, toward the end of his life, he consumed two pigeons, three steaks, and most of four bottles of wine and liquor.

At *breakfast*.

By the time Tambora erupted, the debts of the prince regent had reached the incredible total of £1,480,600—the equivalent today of some $60 million.

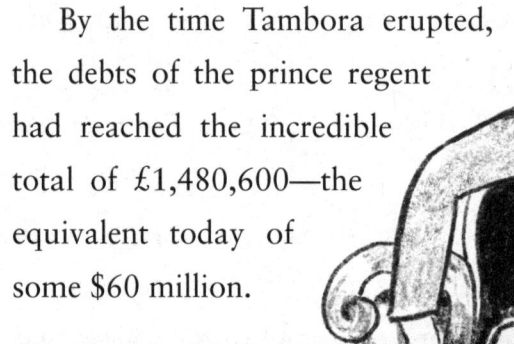

In the spring of 1816, while the Tambora crisis was fast becoming apparent, the English Parliament celebrated the wedding of the prince's daughter. She was awarded—in today's money—an annual sum of $1 million for *jewelry alone.*

At around the same time, the English government received the results of a quarterly survey of farmers. In normal times, this was a dull document. But these were not normal times, and the survey was so pessimistic that the government feared civic unrest if it was made public. They printed as few copies as possible and designated those secret.

If things were as dire as the survey indicated, the government might not last the year. The whole English system—the ill king, the rakish prince, the impotent Parliament—might lose their heads. They might be sent to the gallows. It had happened a few decades before in Paris, when something as seemingly minor as a shortage of bread helped spark the French Revolution. An agricultural crisis—a shift in the weather—could bring down a government. It could convulse a whole society.

The French Revolution was still recent, and bloody, history.

Its legacy was like the bloodred snow in Italy.

It was a sign.

---◇---

Across the English Channel, the winter in Europe had been bearable, bad but bearable. There was the small matter of the multicolored snow, which was disturbing, but that had stopped falling and the rain had started, which was normal.

Then the rain hadn't stopped, which was not.

Europe was a continent that desperately wanted a return to normal. It was ill-equipped to survive a crisis. It just had, after all. Of all men born in France between 1790 and 1795, a stunning one in five had died in the Napoleonic Wars. The country was deep in debt; it had borrowed extravagantly to finance Napoléon's war. But it had lost that war, and the winners required France to repay the massive sums *they'd* spent fighting.

France was a nation mired in the mistakes of the past.

It had no room for a terrible present.

It slowly became clear, however, that that was what it had. Because the rains did not stop.

Rain is the least impressive of disasters. It has none of the drama of a hurricane, or the suddenness of a tornado, or the intensity of a heat wave. It's just rain. *Again.* It happens to us, too, and when it does, we sound like the farmer that spring in Alsace, on the border between France and Germany, complaining in his diary: "The rainy weather continues."

But too much of anything, even something as mundane as rain, can be calamitous.

Which is why the Alsatian farmer then wrote: "The grass is rotting on the meadows, all the mountains are full of water. There is nothing but misery everywhere."

Fields became rivers. Meadows became lakes.

Soon, the Seine—the river that cuts through Paris—would rise, and rise, and rise. It would rise some eight feet in only a few days, higher than any person on its bank.

The storms were relentless. In Germany a storm was "so violent" it tore off roofs and toppled "heavily laden wagons and uprooted 36,000 trees" in the woods around a single town. This wasn't a notable storm. It was just a storm, picked here more or less at random, chosen from the daily calamities as the calendar of 1816 worked its way toward summer.

A supposed summer.

That spring, there were few countries as vulnerable as Switzerland. In the years before Tambora, whole villages there had been impoverished by the arrival of the mechanical loom, which had put an end to the artisanal work of hand-spinning yarn. So when the veil from Tambora took shape overhead, tens of thousands in Switzerland were already out of work. If things got worse for them, there was no safety net—there was nothing to catch their fall.

And still the rain came down.

———◇———

Meanwhile, Mary Godwin was crossing over to France.

She was leaving England behind. She was leaving its clouds, its rain, its rumors. There were many rumors now, and they were about her, and they were cruel. She was no longer a beautiful, brilliant child. She was a walking scandal, who'd betrayed all the norms of polite society.

So she was heading for somewhere better, somewhere beautiful, somewhere *sunny*.

She was heading for Switzerland.

SOME QUESTIONS FOR THE READER, ALSO KNOWN AS YOU, PART II

Is this too much weather?

There's a fair amount of rain here.

Fine, there's a lot of rain.

So much rain.

And before that, a lot of volcano.

Volcanoes roar. They growl. They rumble.

But they don't talk.

We expect our characters to be able to talk.

———◇———

Most of the time, we humans put ourselves at the center of our stories. We put our actual selves there, if we can manage it, but at the very least we put other humans there.

We make ourselves the main characters.

We don't make a *volcano* a character. We don't make *rain* a character.

But there's a danger to telling stories that way.

Because if the story of Tambora tells us anything, it is this: we're not the main character.

———◇———

Zoom out and you can see the main character, though.

You have to zoom *way* out, hundreds of miles out, thousands of miles out. Get on a spaceship if you need to.

Then look back.

There should be a round, blue ball back there somewhere.

That's it. That's the main character. It's always the main character.

———◇———

Now zoom in, *way* in. Find the icy white peaks of Switzerland. Find the placid blue of Lake Geneva. Find a young woman with strawberry hair.

(Did we forget to say you should go back two hundred years? Go back two hundred years.)

That's Mary Godwin.

She probably looks wet.

A LIFE WITHOUT COMPROMISE

SWITZERLAND AND ENGLAND
1814–1816

SNOW AND SCANDAL

In May of 1816, on the eve of the worst summer ever known in Switzerland, Mary Godwin checked into the Hôtel d'Angleterre on the shore of Lake Geneva.

She was with Jane, her stepsister, now known as Claire, who was no longer the silly girl who'd hidden behind the sofa with Mary. Claire had drive and desire, and she was why they were in Geneva, instead of Italy, where Mary had wanted to go.

But it wasn't just Mary and Claire.

There was William, Mary's son, born only a few months before.

And there was Percy Shelley, William's father.

The Hôtel d'Angleterre was *the* hotel for English tourists. It had standards. It had expectations.

So when Percy signed into the hotel register, he lied.

Mary, he wrote, was his wife.

Percy had walked into Mary's life a couple of years earlier.

For both, his arrival was an eruption on the scale of Tambora: it changed everything.

He'd come to her house to see William Godwin, Mary's father. Percy idolized William, but then he saw Mary, and the course of his visit changed.

The course of his life changed.

Percy Shelley was a young aristocrat, but he was like few other aristocrats. His political beliefs—he rejected the idea of government—and his religious beliefs—he rejected the idea of God—were so radical they could not be published. But these beliefs were embedded in his poetry, which was already attracting attention.

Percy was a lot like Mary's father, in other words: he had tremendous literary gifts, and he was determined to live life his way, unconstrained by expectation.

(He also already had a wife, Harriet, and a daughter, Eliza. To Percy, this was a small matter.)

Shortly after Percy and Mary met—perhaps the moment they met—Percy was enraptured. Mary was young, radiant, brilliant. Within weeks, he passed her a poem for her eyes only. It made plain his heart.

Mary was smitten. Percy promised a life of passion, a utopian life, a life without compromise.

Percy declared his love for Mary to William Godwin, who was shocked. Godwin was famous for his own radical beliefs;

he'd written of the insignificance of marriage. But talking or writing about such things—that was fine. It was quite another thing to actually *apply* those beliefs.

To apply those beliefs would mean that Mary would be ostracized. If his daughter was associated with the already married Percy Shelley, she'd be cut out of society, even literary society. His extraordinary daughter would be without a future.

Godwin grounded Mary like the teenager she was. She was confined to the upstairs of the house. She stayed there for almost a month, communicating with Percy through letters and books smuggled into the house by Claire.

After weeks of this, Percy sent Mary a note in the dark of night: *A coach is waiting outside.*

All she had to do was sneak down the stairs and elope with him.

She did.

It was the end of July 1814—a couple of years before Tambora.

Mary was just sixteen.

They eloped to France, but they had few plans and less money. Soon they were back in England, where they were widely shunned and where Mary gave birth to a baby who did not survive. The loss was profound. In the months that followed, her thoughts always circled back to the same point: "that I was a mother & am so no longer." Mary dreamed that the baby had come "to life again—that it had only been cold & that we rubbed it by the fire & it lived—I awake & find no baby." Before long, she was pregnant again, and this child, William, lived.

Mary and Percy were constantly short of money, and so they were constantly moving, or discussing whether to move, or discussing where to move. They were shut out of polite society, or pretty much any society at all. Even Mary's own father refused to see her. By eloping, she had become a scandal. At the time, a single impulsive act could stain your reputation indelibly, at least if you were a woman, and Mary would carry the taint all her life.

It was at this point—May of 1816—that all of them, including Claire, slipped out of England without notice. Mary's father was not told; neither was Percy's wife. (Yes, Percy was still married.)

After a few days in Paris, they headed for Geneva to meet a man named Lord Byron. The name was already legendary: like Percy, Byron was an extraordinary poet and a scandalous aristocrat. He was also the love interest of Claire, who'd had a secret affair with him and was eager to see him again.

It was a dismal trip. The French were sullen, the journey to Switzerland hard, the weather uniformly miserable. "The spring, as the inhabitants informed us, was unusually late," Mary wrote, "and indeed the cold was excessive." Rain fell on their carriage. As they rose in the mountains, snow pelted the windows. It was May, and yet the road was frozen.

They'd had it with the weather. They were so desperate they left the mountain village of Les Rousses for Geneva at dusk. It was a colossally bad idea. Snow was falling along with the temperature. For this final push, they required a closed carriage with no fewer than four horses and ten men. The horses were for pulling the carriage up the steep paths. But the horses could not always stay on the icy paths, and that's why the men were there: for pulling the carriage out of the snowdrifts.

Finally, from a mountain pass, the clouds cleared. A view opened up, a vertiginous view.

Mary looked down. Finally, here would be the beauty of Switzerland, the Alps, the famous Lake Geneva, the—

Below her was an unhappy mixture of clouds and snow, a barren landscape made by Tambora.

"Never," she wrote later, "was a scene more awfully desolate."

FROZEN FEET AND FROZEN BIRDS

THE UNITED STATES
1816

WHAT IS TO BECOME
OF THIS COUNTRY

Across the Atlantic, the United States had escaped the Napoleonic Wars, but it hadn't escaped war.

Its War of 1812 had ended just before Tambora erupted. It had been a battle against Great Britain, a sort of second Revolutionary War, and there was no winner this time, not really. But it proved that the American victory in the Revolutionary War was not a fluke. It had once again held its own against Great Britain.

No one knew that there was a different sort of battle on the horizon.

On February 27, 1816—almost exactly a year after the treaty that ended the War of 1812—the *New York Evening Post* published an article taken from the *Java Government Gazette*. It was a "full and interesting account" of a recent volcanic eruption in the region.

It was Tambora.

This story, buried amid theatrical announcements and ship arrivals, was the key that would unlock the mysteries of the awful coming year.

No one would find it.

———◇———

As in Europe, so in America: the new year of 1816 began flush with promise. The war was over; the land would flourish.

The year, however, did not want to begin.

It was spring on the calendar, but not outside. March was cold, and April was cold, too, and that was fine, that was nothing new. But in May, the ground in New Hampshire was "so cold and wet" it couldn't be worked. The fields were iced over. In many places, there was still snow a half foot deep. New England could be this chilly in May, even if it rarely was.

But then the cold front went south. Into Maryland, where snow fell that was red and blue—patriotic snow. Into Tennessee, where cotton dropped from its stalks, frozen. Into Virginia, where farmers were forced to replant whole fields.

"Everyone complains of the present 'strange weather; this unnatural weather; this unseasonable weather,'" a newspaper in Pennsylvania reported.

As May became June, the season finally changed. But now it was too hot: the temperatures soared into the hundreds, even in New England. The normal working of the skies was out of order, and so the weather became bizarrely random. Suddenly, the insufferably hot days cooled as if plunged into an ice bath: a storm sent thermometers down forty degrees in a day, and then by that same amount the next day. Highs, not lows, were in the twenties.

This storm arrived with terrifying speed, and it was not a cold snap, not a light frost. It was snow, thick snow. Parts of Massachusetts saw a foot. In Vermont, some eighteen inches fell. The snow was so deep a man who'd gone for a walk could not find his way back. After a night outside, his feet froze through. He lost a toe. Another Vermont man did not survive at all.

He'd died of exposure in the *summer*.

———◇———

For those days in June—a stretch that must have felt like weeks—all of New England froze. Fires were made. Coats were found.

"Probably no one living in the country ever witnessed such weather," reported a Vermont newspaper. From Maine: "What is to become of this country, it is impossible to divine— distressing beyond description."

The sheep had just been sheared, so their fleece was tied back on, like sweaters. Sheep are not meant to wear sweaters. They froze.

The birds froze, too. They fell from trees, hard and cold. When they flew inside houses for warmth, they were so numb and numerous a person could pick them up by the handful.

Whole fields, newly replanted after the May frost, withered.

None of it made sense. The world had emerged from winter, only to turn around and walk back into it.

"Not a green leaf is to be seen for acres together," a New Jersey newspaper reported. "The oldest person here has no recollection of a like season."

But summer would come soon.

It *had* to come.

HOPES FELL FAST

But what if it didn't?

What if this still new United States had done something to anger the heavens above?

It seemed altogether possible. Because the next frigid wave arrived—with uncanny timing—on the Fourth of July.

The parades were held in sunshine, but the sun held no warmth. People celebrated in thick overcoats, while their wells froze over.

Walking to work a few days after the holiday, a young New England watchmaker was so cold "that I was obliged to lay down my tools and put on a pair of mittens which I had in my pocket." It would soon start snowing. The day was so odd that the man would remember it the rest of his long life.

There was a new worry, too: not only was there no warmth, there was no rain. The only moisture that seemed to fall was snow, which was not helpful.

This was the topsy-turvy world made by Tambora. The rain in Europe would not stop. In the United States, it would not *start*.

Drought set in.

Fields that had been frozen were now dry.

———◇———

These were not the farms of today, with crops neatly planted out to the horizon.

They were smaller, rougher, far more varied.

We think of early America as a land of farmers. But we should think of it as a land of *gardeners*.

In 1816, the United States was at a tipping point. It was about to become a land of commerce and industry. But it was not yet. The economy of America had not changed significantly in a century. People were still subsistence farmers—they farmed to survive, not to earn money. The small amount they sold only added up to a small income. People bartered rather than bought.

If the crops failed, a family had no good options. Few could afford to buy food, because few were working for money. There wasn't much food to buy, anyway, because most everyone grew what they ate and ate what they grew.

And in 1816, in field after field, in garden after garden, the crops failed.

At the end of July, the weather improved. Hopes rose.

The cold had been a trial, many said, but America had lived through it. The country was still in the good graces of God.

And then—then it all happened again.

At the height of summer, at the moment when crops should be heavy and ripe, the cold came again, and again, and again: "August was proved to be the worst month of all." In Washington, DC, a city famous for sweltering summers, there was ice on the Potomac River. In Virginia, the frost was "a circumstance unparalleled in this part of the country, and what is equally extraordinary, we have had frost every month during the year."

Hopes fell fast. Rain fell not at all.

The drought was severe. In New England, month after month passed without rain. In Philadelphia, the Schuylkill River was so low a person could cross it without getting their feet wet—the very opposite of the rivers of Europe, which were overflowing.

Across America, congregations fasted. They went without food to persuade God of the depth of their devotion. But some looked elsewhere for an explanation. Had they been less devoted to God this year? They had not. Had they been more sinful? They had not. Had the weather been worse nonetheless? It had.

People seemed to sense that something strange, something *new* was happening. They did not know it was a climate shock—they didn't have that vocabulary—but they did go looking for a different sort of vocabulary: they went in search of an explanation outside the language of *sin* and *punishment*.

As it happened, there were explanations out there.

There were many, many explanations.

And they were all wrong.

(Almost.)

MANY WRONGS DO NOT MAKE A RIGHT

THE WORLD
1816

THE FIRST
WRONG

The sunspots were just a curiosity, at first. The dark blotches on the sun had been visible in the winter, but only the astronomers had cared.

So no one worried, not at first.

The worry came later.

The worry came as the seasons failed to change. Suddenly, there were more sunspots, and there was no spring, and it was easy to believe that the two might be connected.

Plus, the spots were large, weirdly large. They could be seen without a telescope. They became such a sensation that pieces of colored glass were sold so that people could examine the spots safely.

Also, they grew. An especially large sunspot hovered through early May, and although it might be harmless, it *was* weird. And as long as the weather was weird, too, it seemed

weirder. More people looked up. More people wondered what was happening up there.

They worried. We know that they worried because many newspapers spent a lot of time telling their readers *not* to worry.

The sunspots were normal, the stories said.

Normal!

Besides, they were harmless.

Normal! Harmless!

In fact, they were helpful, because good harvests often followed sunspots.

Normal! Harmless! Helpful!

Also, they were beautiful.

Normal! Harmless! Helpful! Beautiful!

This did not work. Suspicions grew. The authorities were now worried, too, although not about the sunspots. They were worried about their own citizens. A disturbed population was not a docile population. There was talk that the sunspots would extinguish the sun, and if the sun was extinguished, life on Earth would be, too. If people had nothing to live for—if they thought the world was ending—they might revolt.

The French government treated the matter with grave concern. It printed and distributed pamphlets stressing that the sunspots would change nothing about the sun. A French philosopher gave public lectures on the sunspots "in order to convince the credulous that there need be no fear of the extinction of that luminary, and consequently that the world is not speedily coming to an end; as reported by many malevolent and superstitious persons."

But many people on both sides of the Atlantic were unconvinced. The weather was simply too weird. "The philosophers assure us there is nothing to be apprehended from the spots on the sun," wrote a Boston newspaper, "but by a strange coincidence, the coldness of the present season, both in Europe and America, has chilled the earth at the very period when those spots were largest and occurred most frequently." It was "at least worthy of remark," a different Boston newspaper noted, that sunspots, "each time, have been preceded by an extraordinary change in the weather."

By the summer, the spots had increased in size and number. Each new sunspot made the papers, which analyzed each in precise detail. The sun was said to be like a piece of cloth "in a thread-bare state," and by September, its "cheeks" were "all covered with spots." They spread across the sphere like "black bile."

The sun was sick, a French doctor announced, and the moon would soon be dead.

Some feared that the spots would keep increasing in size and number. If they did, the sun would become "wholly incrusted" with spots and the earth would be plunged into "unutterable darkness."

The sun would become a sunspot.

Even the future American president John Quincy Adams, a man of deep faith in science, was not sure what to think. It was true that the weather was feeble and the sun seemingly defective. "What agency the spots in the sun have had in all this," he wrote his mother from London, "is more than I, or perhaps anybody else is astronomer enough to know."

Meanwhile, the spots kept erupting, splitting, combining.

A worried world squinted skyward.

THE SECOND WRONG

There was something else strange up above. It wasn't on the sun, though. It was on the tops of buildings—there were long rods of metal there, stretching upward.

They hadn't always been there. They were there now because, decades before Tambora, Benjamin Franklin—the American scientist and revolutionary—had tamed the skies.

He'd realized that a metal rod placed on top of buildings could attract lightning and that light-ning could be

safely directed toward the ground without damage or injury. Before Franklin, buildings were at serious risk from lightning strikes, a common cause of fires. After Franklin, they were safe.

He'd invented the lightning rod—a wondrous, paradoxical thing.

It was brilliant. But it was new and it was strange, so it was suspect. Lightning was a mystical, terrifying force. Many assumed it was a divine force. It seemed beyond the power of humans to manage it.

And so when the weather went awry, some said it was because the lightning rods were messing with the weather. It was worse than that, actually: the lightning rods were messing with divine forces.

There were more theories, too. Maybe the lightning rods were draining the atmosphere of heat. Maybe they were creating more clouds and rain. The details of these theories weren't important—and there weren't many details. They were theories driven by fear, not logic. What mattered was their conclusion: by disrupting lightning, Benjamin Franklin had altered the normal course of electricity. From the grave, he'd managed an unlikely feat: he was responsible for a wave of horrible weather.

And so in Germany and Switzerland, across Central Europe, lightning rods were ripped from the tops of buildings.

THE THIRD
WRONG

Or maybe these explanations—the sunspots and the lightning rods—were aimed in the wrong direction. Maybe the problem wasn't up above.

Maybe it was down below.

In the winter of 1811, a series of devastating earthquakes shook the region where Illinois, Missouri, and Tennessee now come together. These were major quakes, registering toward the top of the Richter scale, the yardstick for earthquakes. They sent the Mississippi River running backward. They split the soil apart and sucked it down, leaving only the smell of sulfur behind.

The terror of these earthquakes was still fresh when the weather turned weird. It was inevitable that someone would connect the events, and many did.

A new theory was proposed: the haywire weather was coming from *inside* the earth.

There was electrical fluid underneath the surface of the earth, according to this theory. The circulation of that fluid generated heat, but the earthquakes had altered it. Therefore, the normal exchange of electricity between the earth and the atmosphere was awry and thus the weather was, too.

In a sort of accidental way, the theory was absolutely correct. The weird weather *had* come from deep inside the earth, from far below Tambora, from the shifting tectonic plates.

But in every other way, the theory was wrong. No part of it was correct: not the electrical fluid, not the heat, not the earthquakes altering the circulation (which wasn't circulating anyway, because there was no electrical fluid to circulate). For theorizing purposes, earthquakes had the same advantages as sunspots: no one understood either, so they could be interpreted in as wild a way as could be imagined.

They were strange and new, and the weather was strange and new, so it was at least an explanation. Any explanation was seized on.

And there were so many explanations.

THE MANY, MANY, MANY OTHER WRONGS

The icebergs in the Arctic. (Which were cooling Europe.)

The rice paddies in Italy. (Which were fouling the skies.)

The logged forests in France. (Which were altering the balance of nature.)

There were more theories; there were so many theories.

The recent lunar eclipse.

The recent *solar* eclipse.

The sudden end of the Napoleonic Wars. A German scholar proposed that the gunpowder from the wars had blocked the cold currents from the Arctic. Now the gunpowder was gone, and so the Arctic cold was back. The only way to restore the climate was to go to war again.

And why not?

It may have seemed as likely as anything else.

As likely as sunspots, as lightning rods, as earthquakes.

If anyone had proposed a volcano halfway around the world, *that* would have seemed unlikely.

That would have seemed preposterous.

Which makes it all the more remarkable that someone had proposed it, decades before.

AND A
RIGHT

1783. ICELAND.

Like Indonesia, Iceland was made by volcanoes. It is a land of ice, yes, but it is also a land of fire. Its sagas sing of volcanic scenes straight from Tambora:

> The sun begins to be dark; the continent
>   falls fainting into the Ocean
> They disappear from the sky, the brilliant stars
> The smoke eddies around the destroying
>   fire of the world
> The gigantic flame plays against heaven itself.

But Iceland had never seen a volcano like Laki.
No one had.

There were weeks of earthquakes before the rift opened in an Icelandic valley and the underworld came into the light. Fire rose a half mile into the air, wreathed in black haze.

Lava poured out with a speed and quantity that are still unmatched. At its peak, Laki released the equivalent of a pair of Olympic-sized swimming pools of lava every second.

For weeks.

In the words of an Icelandic pastor unfortunate enough to be there: "First the Earth swelled up, with a chorus of howls, filled with an uproar that made it explode into pieces, tore it apart and eviscerated it like a rabid animal rips something to pieces."

A line of fissures formed, ripping apart the land on either side of Laki.

A quarter of Iceland perished.

But the fallout went far beyond this lonely island.

Laki was a very sulfuric volcano, and within a week, Europe noticed something amiss. The smoky fog, wrote an English naturalist, was "unlike anything known within the memory of man."

The haze, reeking of sulfur, smothered Europe. Breathing was difficult. Coughing was constant. In the winter, seemingly all the continent froze; in the spring, when the thaw came, the floods were prodigious.

No one knew the source of the haze, and rumor abounded. The mystery attracted the attention of Benjamin Franklin, then the United States ambassador to France. The weather had been anomalous, Franklin noted in a letter to a friend in Manchester, England, and the fog was so thick that "the rays of the sun seemed to have little effect towards dissipating it." Franklin being Franklin, he conducted an experiment, focusing those "diminished" rays

in a magnifying glass and aiming the beam at a piece of paper. The paper failed to burn. So the sunlight *was* weaker. Franklin admitted that the reason was not "ascertained," but he had theories. It was possible—and Franklin saved this theory for last—that the cause was "the vast quantity of smoke continuing to issue" from the volcano known to be erupting in Iceland. Perhaps the hard winter had also been the result of this eruption, and perhaps previous hard winters in history had stemmed from similar eruptions.

A few months later, Franklin's musings were read aloud to the Manchester Literary and Philosophical Society. They were written down and published. While finalizing the peace treaty that ended the Revolutionary War, Benjamin Franklin had connected volcanoes with climate change.

No one paid any attention.

The haze from Laki lifted.

The crisis came to a close.

And when the weather went berserk after Tambora, thirty years later, no one would find the trail that Benjamin Franklin had already laid.

They blamed his lightning rods instead.

SOME QUESTIONS FOR THE READER, ALSO KNOWN AS YOU, PART III

Those who lived through the Tambora years had all the clues already. The skies were hazy, the weather was bizarre. Everyone could see that. It wasn't a secret.

The problem was they didn't know how to make sense of it. They didn't know how to *interpret* it.

The idea that some people were better than others at interpreting things—that was a new concept. It's the idea of expertise, and the whole notion of expertise was still being worked out. William Herschel was the great astronomer of the day, a deeply learned man, and yet his views about sunspots were not taken much more seriously than the views of the man who'd heard something from somebody who'd heard something from somebody who'd heard that the sun was going out the day after tomorrow.

All the evidence from the Tambora years didn't add up to anything. It just inspired wild guesses about earthquakes and lightning rods and rice paddies. This is the fate of a world without the idea of expertise, a world without any sense of whom to trust. In that world, *any* story was a relief. It's not a surprise that people migrated from explanation to explanation to explanation.

Any story was better than nothing at all.

———◇———

So would it have mattered if someone had found Benjamin Franklin's dusty speculation in the *Memoirs of the Literary and Philosophical Society of Manchester*?

Would it have mattered if someone else had proposed Tambora as the cause?

Would anyone have listened?

SOME ATE SOIL

THE WORLD
1816 AND THE YEARS THAT FOLLOWED

CLAY AND CHOLERA

Some people didn't go looking for an explanation, because they didn't need anything explained. As far as they knew, the world was humming along smoothly.

This was the randomness of Tambora: sun here, agony there.

But *randomness* is the wrong word, really.

Because this is what a climate shock does. The weather does its work in well-worn grooves, but when it spins out of those grooves, it can spiral in many directions. Climate change can be brutally unfair: catastrophic for some, bearable for others.

The Russian Empire was not far from the miseries of this story. But it would emerge from Tambora unscathed. In fact, the good harvest there would save Europe from far greater miseries.

No one in Russia was afraid of the sunspots, because there was no reason to be afraid of anything.

We know the most about Tambora's fallout in the United States and in Europe—the record of its damage is deepest in those places. A global story like Tambora is always tilted unfairly. It's tilted in favor of who wrote what down where and whose writings were preserved.

But we do know that Tambora's fallout was not limited to the United States and Europe. It's very possible that those regions didn't even suffer the worst consequences.

We know that in southern Africa, Tambora shifted the weather patterns, ushering in a period of cold and drought that were deeply destabilizing. The years after Tambora are called the Mfecane, and they were a time of prolonged famine and conflict.

We know that Brazil was deep in drought, too, and that a large part of that very large country was in serious distress: "All the streams had been dried up, the cattle were dying or dead, and all the population emigrating to the borders of the great rivers in search of water."

We know that China suffered a catastrophe. And perhaps nowhere there was harder hit than the beautiful province of Yunnan.

The climate of Yunnan is normally mild, with rich soil and mountainsides terraced with rice. Yunnan is famous for sun—its Chinese name means *south of the cloud*—but in the years after Tambora, the sun never dawned there.

Yunnan was no longer south of the cloud. It was *in* the cloud.

The growing season shrank to nothing. It was never warm, and rice cannot survive even moderate cold. The harvest failed.

The winter of the year after Tambora, some in Yunnan were so desperate they ate the clay soil.

The next summer, there was no sun again.

Instead, there was *snow*. The water in the rice paddies froze. The harvest failed.

That winter, some ate soil again.

Some parents in Yunnan sold their children into slavery. The choice was slavery or death, and anyone who bought their child would at least feed their child.

It was the same tragic, unthinkable calculation made on the beaches outside Tambora.

———◆———

In India, the year after Tambora, the monsoon was late.

The monsoon was the lifeblood of the region, a massive storm that lasted for the summer months and supplied the vast majority of rain. But it had to be the right amount of rain and it had to be at the right time.

And it was not at the right time.

Also, the skies were strange. There was a "thick, 'heavy' state of the air, giving it a *whitish* appearance." No one knew why.

And still the monsoon did not come.

The monsoon has an almost mythic reputation, but its origins are simple: it is sparked when the land heats up faster than the water surrounding it. The difference between those

temperatures fuels the monsoon: the hot air over the land rises and the cool air from the ocean takes its place. The winds are wild and they are soaked with moisture from the sea.

But after Tambora, the Indian subcontinent stayed cool, and so the monsoon was late.

The seasons had been jarred loose. Nothing arrived on schedule and nothing arrived in the right amounts. When the sun shone, there was too much of it. The heat was unbearable. Whole rivers were dust. When the rainy season came the next year, it was too early and it did not leave. Whole regions were underwater.

The rains were especially severe around what today is Bangladesh, where the sudden shift in the monsoon had catastrophic consequences. A deadly, disease-causing microbe named cholera had lived there for likely thousands of years. It was contained. Outbreaks of cholera only occurred seasonally and locally.

But when the seasons were altered, cholera was as well. It adapted to the new conditions. The seasons were no longer normal, and so cholera was no longer seasonal. Within months it leapt out of its native river habitat and tore across India, a tidal wave of death.

Let's zoom out. Because cholera did not stop there. It continued to spread. It traveled across Asia, where it killed as many people in Indonesia as Tambora had initially. It moved across the Middle East and into Africa. It slowed its pace and then picked up terrifying speed. Like some sort of apocalyptic sightseer, it ran through Moscow in 1829, Paris in 1830, London in 1831, New York in 1832. Many millions would die, and those deaths can be laid at the slopes of Tambora. Its eruption altered the climate, and that altered climate let loose a new phenomenon: a climate change disease.

But all this lay in the future. No one in 1816 anticipated this wave of misery. They were too consumed by their own.

BREAD
OR BLOOD

ENGLAND AND EUROPE
1816

WE MUST HAVE
FLOUR CHEAPER

To see the sunspots in Europe, in the spring of 1816, you had to find space between the clouds. The rain was still coming down.

In Copenhagen, Denmark's capital, it fell very nearly every day for five weeks.

In Germany, farmers were in "utter despair," laboring through "continual rains, torrents the like of which we have never before seen, storms followed by hail."

In the English countryside, boats sailed on meadows. In Switzerland, rivers were so high that boats passed *over* bridges.

It was now summer, but there was no summer to be found.

"During the entire season the sun rose each morning as though in a cloud of smoke," an English clergyman wrote, "red and rayless, shedding little light or warmth and setting at night behind a thick cloud of vapor, leaving hardly a trace of its having passed over the face of the earth."

The *Times* of London reported that "such an inclement summer is scarcely remembered by the oldest inhabitant of London or its environs." This was a generous interpretation: it suggested there *had* been a summer. A more straightforward interpretation came years later: "Rural England in 1816 descended into a land of the living dead."

———◇———

Thousands of soldiers had come home to England after the Napoleonic Wars, a torrent of restless men.

For many, there was nothing to do. In the cities, there was little work. In the countryside, there was less, and the work was newly humiliating.

In rural England, the poor once had a measure of liberty: access to a common garden and pasture, which was a source of food and profit outside of work. That world was now gone. The English countryside had been carved up into private parcels of land.

Without anywhere to graze animals or grow food, workers were left with a pair of bad options. On farms, they would be paid little and worked without end: when the summer was high, from four in the morning to eight in the evening. In factories—the new industrial world—they'd suffer the same indignities. They would not choose their schedules or even their work. They would be subject to the rules and whims of others. In either place, they would be dependent, wholly dependent, and it would get them nowhere. "Practically every

A crowd assembled in the marketplace with red-and-white flags. They'd brought a paper with their demands. These were simple: BREAD OR BLOOD.

A local judge met with the crowd, which was apologetic but earnest. A protestor explained that he did not mean any harm, but "he could not live with his large family as things were, *and they must have flour cheaper.*"

The crowd returned the following day, this time well over a thousand strong, carrying sticks and spikes. The paper was now a banner: BREAD OR BLOOD.

The protestors felt—very reasonably—that everyone was against them. They'd been oppressed by the government, the clergy, the landowners, the farmers. There was no one who had their interests in mind.

Therefore: everyone was fair game.

Riots broke out, and they are heartbreaking to read about.

There is drunkenness. There is property damage: windows smashed, buildings burned. There is theft: beer, beef, bread. There are threats of violence, although there is little actual violence.

That's not the heartbreaking part.

The heartbreaking part is that after all this—after defying the demands of the authorities, after risking their lives, after *rioting,* which was a crime that came with a potential death sentence—after all this, their demands were so small. They didn't want to overthrow the government. They wanted to be able to *afford food.* Their solution was simple: either wages should be higher or bread should be cheaper.

A settlement was worked out between the local authorities and the protestors: workers should be paid a certain amount when flour was cheap and more when flour was expensive.

That was it, essentially.

That was the agreement it had required violence to bring into being. And it was a paltry agreement, backed by nothing but a promise.

A promise that would not be kept.

The protestors asked for forgiveness, too—protection from prosecution. They were given it.

That promise would not be kept, either.

Another protest marched through another town a few days later. The local clergyman tried to persuade the small group of protestors to disband. He did not succeed. "So help me, God," a protestor said in response. "I would sooner lose my life than go home as I am. Bread I want and bread I will have."

The riots were over almost as soon as they started. Afterward, there were trials. Five men were hanged. Many more were sentenced to prison or transport to Australia, which was then used by Great Britain as a prison. It was a voyage often equivalent to death.

It had all been for nothing, or perhaps it had all been for exactly what the banner had said: bread.

They hadn't gotten a loaf.

They hadn't gotten half a loaf.

They'd gotten none.

———◇———

In England, these uprisings were the most sizable since the time of the French Revolution.

They terrified the authorities, who knew exactly what had happened in the French Revolution.

All this was before the harvest.

A harvest the English government already knew would be disastrous.

Which was news they were already trying to suppress.

———◇———

In response, the English Parliament decided to do nothing.

Almost nothing, anyway. They distributed small amounts of relief, but that was it. Soldiers adjusting to home would have to adjust; farmers coping with the weather would have to cope.

The only remedy, the leader of the House of Commons announced, would be "the healing influence of time."

In response, the prince regent took the floor of Parliament. First, he thanked the Parliament for their "cordial interest" in the wedding of his daughter and gave the "warmest acknowledgments" for their support. Then he announced the upcoming wedding of his sister and hoped that the event would be "highly gratifying" to his subjects. Only at the end of his speech did he admit that there was "distress" in the land.

It did not trouble him, however. The prince relied "with perfect confidence" on the "public spirit and fortitude" of his subjects in rising above their current difficulties.

Then he adjourned Parliament for a month.

When his sister was married a few weeks later, there were goblets of pure gold on the altar.

THIS EXTRAORDINARY TERROR

Perhaps none of this would matter, however.

Because the end of the world was nigh.

This news had come from the Italian scholarly city of Bologna. An astronomer there had been observing the sunspots. He'd come to a modest conclusion, according to the London *Morning Chronicle:* "On the 18th of July a great solar catastrophe is to put an end to the world by conflagration." The *Morning Chronicle* added: "The Government, thinking it improper to suffer the circulation of such predictions, has put the astronomer under arrest."

The government was worried because the prediction was so easy to believe. The sun looked different. It *felt* different.

The astronomer was locked up, but his prophecy was free. Townspeople throughout Austria assembled in such numbers that the military was called in. In the English town of Bath, a girl "woke her aunt and shouted at her that the world was ending." The aunt "plunged into a coma." A maid in London hanged herself.

In Liège, Belgium, a "huge cloud in the shape of a mountain" put the town on high alert. On the other side of Belgium, a military regiment, riding through a town during a thunderstorm, blew their trumpets. The thunder, the lightning, the peal of the trumpets: it was all too much. Some "three-quarters of the inhabitants" rushed outside and threw "themselves on their knees on the streets." They were already expecting the end of the world, and so when the trumpets blared, they thought they'd heard the seven trumpets from the Book of Revelation in the New Testament, the prelude to the apocalypse. "Suddenly cries, groans, tears, lamentations, were heard on every side," a witness said. "It was not without infinite trouble that the cause of this extraordinary terror was discovered."

People were living inside the end of days. Thoughts were not of this world but the next. The London *Times* wrote: "In France as well as in this country, and generally throughout Europe, the prediction of the mad Italian prophet, relative to the end of the world, had produced great dread in the minds of some, so that they neglected all business, and gave themselves entirely to despondency."

Many called the prophecy foolish and those who believed it ignorant, but calling people ignorant and their beliefs foolish has rarely been convincing, and it did not work this time, either. The London *Times* tried to disprove the prophecy by its own biblical logic: it could not be true because in the Bible "the end of the world is to be announced by the Anti-Christ, and there are yet no accounts of his appearance."

This was both reassuring and distressing. There was no Anti-Christ: that part was good.

But the Anti-Christ might appear at any moment. That part was bad.

In Paris the day before, "the end of the world on the 18th appeared to be a certainty." A pamphlet was published with the title *Détails Sur la fin du Monde*—Details on the End of the World. It sold well.

The world has been scheduled to end many times, yet it somehow never does. But the prophecy was not the point, not really. The point was that it caught fire. An apocalyptic prediction only takes hold when people *want* to believe in it. The Bologna prophecy filled the yawning hole of worry and dread that many felt.

The fact that the prophecy did not come true—that didn't solve the problem.

The worry and dread were still there.

The sun was still spotted. The rain was still torrential. The harvest was still endangered.

Soon, a priest in Naples declared that the city would be decimated only a few days later: "It was to rain fire for four hours; and those who escaped the fire were to be devoured by serpents."

Like the astronomer before him, the priest was locked up.

Lesser prophets took to the streets. A new rumor spread: the sun would not go out, but part of it would *fly off*. The fear that "a piece of the sun would break off and crash into the earth 'gripped all of Europe.'"

It must have felt as likely as anything else.

THE SPARK OF LIFE ITSELF

SWITZERLAND
1816

A HIDEOUS
PHANTASM

Desolate.

That's how Geneva had looked from the mountain pass.

But then Mary Shelley descended, and fortune smiled.

For a few days, she was graced with the rarest prize of that summer: the sun.

Mary and Percy sailed across the lake. They walked in the gardens. They read Latin and Italian together. This was the life they'd imagined: not silly social affairs, but days of sensual delight and intellectual adventure, played out before the most beautiful backdrop in Europe.

They were heady days.

"I feel as happy as a new-fledged bird," Mary wrote in a letter, "and hardly care what twig I fly to, so that I may try my newfound wings."

In many ways, these were the finest days of their lives together. They had no way of knowing.

———◇———

Lord Byron arrived ten days later.

Everyone knew it. For his whole life, whenever Lord Byron did anything—arrived somewhere, left somewhere, said something, said *nothing*—everyone knew it.

Only twenty-eight, Byron was already a celebrity—not famous so much as infamous. He'd left England under the weight of rumor and scandal; he'd been labeled "mad, bad, and dangerous to know." But his poetic gift attracted almost as much attention as his exploits. He was impossible, but he was also brilliant, and everyone at the Hôtel d'Angleterre knew all about him already.

He made it easy. His carriage was designed to resemble Napoléon's, and when it pulled up in Geneva, Byron was with his usual traveling companions: "Eight enormous dogs, three monkeys, five cats, an eagle, a crow, and a falcon."

He woke up the whole hotel.

This was not Byron being extravagant. This was Byron being Byron. The guests of the hotel were lucky he had not brought his peacocks, or geese, or goat, all of which traveled with him occasionally. In college, Byron had kept a bear in his room. In Geneva, he kept his entourage—the dogs, the monkeys, all the rest—in the rooms of the formal Hôtel d'Angleterre.

Byron arrived exhausted—he listed his age in the hotel register as 100—and was annoyed to discover Claire there. They'd had an affair, but now he was not interested in her. He was interested in Percy, though. They would become perhaps the most acclaimed poets of the age, and each recognized the genius of the other. They were soon inseparable. Whenever the weather permitted, they went boating on Lake Geneva, and when the weather did not permit, they concocted plans for the rest of the summer.

These involved moving to a secluded pair of houses on the opposite side of the lake. Even there, though, the group was not safe from scrutiny. Guests at the Hôtel d'Angleterre would spy

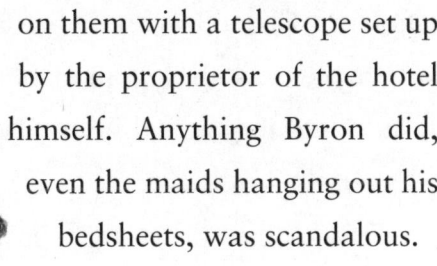

on them with a telescope set up by the proprietor of the hotel himself. Anything Byron did, even the maids hanging out his bedsheets, was scandalous.

Of the houses, Byron's was grander. They gathered there. The mansion, known as Villa Diodati, sat on the hills above the lake, and on clear days, the view was glorious.

The days were not clear.

"Unfortunately we do not now enjoy those brilliant skies that hailed us on our first arrival to this country," Mary wrote shortly after her radiant description of Switzerland. "An almost perpetual rain confines us principally to the house, but when the sun bursts forth it is with a splendor and heat unknown in England."

The weather would not behave. It was temperamental; it was tempestuous: too rainy, and then, all too briefly, too hot. Fog rose across the lake, drawing a curtain over their activities, hiding the party even from telescopes.

They were on their own now, marooned in the fog.

It was just them and Tambora.

———◇———

In those weeks on the far side of Lake Geneva—weeks that would become famous—there was no society. There were no elaborate dinners; there were no grand balls.

There was just weather.

"The thunderstorms that visit us are grander and more terrific than I have ever seen before," Mary wrote in awe. "We watch them as they approach from the opposite side of the lake, observing the lightning play among the clouds in various parts of the heavens."

The weather drove them inside. And so they talked. They

talked all night. They were young, and they were brilliant, and it must have felt like the night lasted forever. "We often sat up in conversation till the morning light," Mary wrote. "There was never any lack of subjects, and, grave or gay, we were always interested."

Meanwhile, the thunder roared over the lake. The lightning cracked across the sky. And inside Villa Diodati, the talk turned to a new theory known as galvanism. Equal parts exhilarating and unnerving, it grew out of the recent discovery that muscles responded to electricity. An experiment had shown that the muscles in an amputated frog leg would contract—as if alive—when an electric current was passed through the leg.

It was evidence of the spark of life itself, a sort of animal electricity that ran through all living beings.

Or at least that was the theory.

"Perhaps a corpse would be reanimated," Mary thought. "Perhaps the component parts of a creature might be manufactured, brought together, and endued with vital warmth."

There was electricity enough outside. "One night we *enjoyed* a finer storm than I had ever before beheld," Mary wrote. "The lake was lit up—the pines on Jura made visible, and all the scene illuminated for an instant, when a pitchy blackness succeeded, and the thunder came in frightful bursts over our heads amid the darkness."

On a dark and stormy night like this, Byron read out loud from a book of horror stories he'd found. But the book wasn't scary enough, or it wasn't literary enough, or it wasn't *enough* enough for Byron. He tossed it aside.

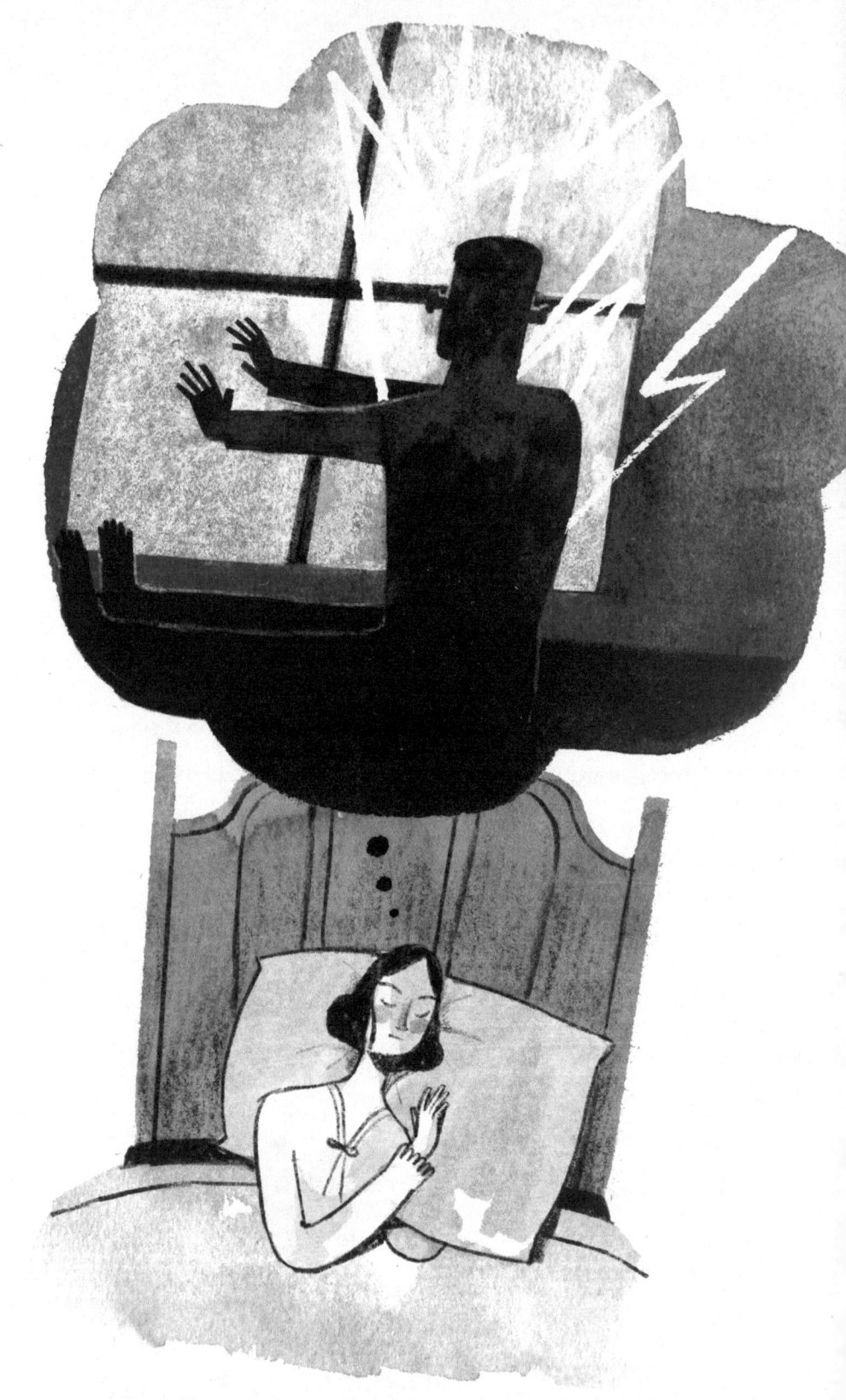

They could do better, he announced. They *would* do better. Everyone there would write their own ghost story—and the best would win. It would be a contest.

For Byron, this was a contest between two people: him and Percy.

Mary wasn't an afterthought.

She wasn't a thought at all.

She was eighteen years old.

She'd never published a thing.

———◇———

"*Have you thought of a story?* I was asked each morning, and each morning I was forced to reply with a mortifying negative."

Each morning, Mary had not. She had not. She—

She had.

The idea arrived in her dreams. She'd found the nightmare in her nightmare: "When I placed my head on my pillow I did not sleep, nor could I be said to think. My imagination, unbidden, possessed and guided me . . .

"I saw—with shut eyes, but acute mental vision—I saw the pale student of unhallowed arts kneeling beside the thing he had put together. I saw the hideous phantasm of a man stretched out, and then, on the working of some powerful engine, show signs of life, and stir with an uneasy, half vital motion."

She'd seen a hideous creature.

Her creature.

I HAD THOUGHT
OF A STORY

By now, Lake Geneva had overflowed its banks.

To live around the lake was to live *in* the lake. "The earth is so prodigiously soaked," a diarist wrote, "that fountains emerge from every hole."

The river running out of the lake carried not just water, but houses, cattle, trees. The streets of Geneva were canals. To get around, locals took boats. A fifteen-pound trout was caught downtown.

This was the upside-down world that Tambora had made. On Sumbawa, what was once the inside—the glowing fire, the hellish sulfates—had turned into the outside. Here in Switzerland, land had turned into water.

And on the shores of Lake Geneva, Mary was stuck inside, stuck in the horrifying vision she'd seen that night.

——◆——

When Mary wrote about her vision years later, she was not just explaining the origins of what would become her masterpiece. She was also explaining how she was capable of writing it. In Regency England, women were not supposed to be writers, but if they were, they were not supposed to be writers of genius.

Mary's vision solved this problem.

She was not a writer of genius. She was the *recipient* of genius.

"I opened [my eyes] in terror," she wrote of her dream. "The idea so possessed my mind that a thrill of fear ran through me."

She lay there, in her room at the foot of the Alps, desperate to leave behind her vision. But she could not: "I could not get rid of my hideous phantom; still it haunted me."

To distract herself, she turned back toward the ghost story competition. "If I could only contrive one which would frighten my reader as I myself had been frightened that night!"

And then it hit her.

"I have found it! What terrified me will terrify others; and I need only describe the specter that haunted my midnight pillow."

Mary was writing in an inside-out landscape, a world that had spun off its axis. If this world was indeed ending, it was not ending well.

And neither would Mary's book.

She had been raised on stories of idealism, dreams of progress. She'd grown up in the home of the most famous idealist of the age. She'd run away with the most famous idealist of the next generation. Those men pursued airy, abstract goals, but she'd had to live with the very real fallout of their choices. The thoughtlessness of Godwin, the irresponsibility of Percy, even the adventurism of Byron—Mary had seen all this up close.

Her life was an education in unforeseen consequences.

Byron and Percy both wrote of heroes—extraordinary individuals with extraordinary powers.

Mary would not imitate their heroic style. She was skeptical of this sort of talk. It was too simple for her, this heroic idealism.

She would write a different sort of book.

Her book would be about the wreckage left behind.

A GOOD YEAR
FOR DREAD

ENGLAND
EUROPE
THE UNITED STATES
HARVEST, 1816

A VERY SHORT LIST OF WHAT GREW IN EUROPE IN 1816

Mud, mostly.

———◇———

To be fair, storms grew, too.

They were relentless. They would have been monotonous, too, except it was never clear what *sort* of bad weather was coming. And they would have been boring, except that winter loomed ahead, and the thought of a winter without a harvest was not boring.

It was terrifying.

In the fields, the snails took up permanent residence. Nothing else liked it there.

By July, word came from Germany that the "hopes of a very fine harvest have been almost ruined." The losses were "incalculable." In August, a storm hit France, sweeping away everything: "The harvest is completely destroyed: wheat, barley, oats, vegetables, vines, and even trees . . ."

Because of the constant rain, there was never a window of good weather to harvest what little had grown. A wet harvest is fine for fruits or vegetables that will be eaten immediately. But for storage crops—the sort of crops that will be milled for flour or fed to animals—it is disastrous.

A wet harvest will mold and rot. Even animals will refuse it.

After the harvest had been delayed again and again, the frosts came early. Farmers who'd held out hope saw their half-grown oats and barley, their meager grains, buried under an icy blanket.

It was a year, a correspondent in England wrote, "having neither spring, nor summer, nor harvest."

———◇———

But Friedrich Wilhelm Karl grew.

He was the king of Württemberg, a territory on the edge of Switzerland, where the whole summer had "felt like November." The little that had grown was killed by an October frost. It was followed by a snowstorm.

In this land where the population was on the edge of famine, King Friedrich Wilhelm Karl kept eating.

He was famous for it. Napoléon had once theorized that God had created the king to show "how far human skin could stretch without bursting."

When the king was not eating, he took time to buy a rhinoceros for the royal zoo.

Not to be outdone, England's prince regent ate and drank himself into a swollen stupor.

But this was too much, even for him.

The doctors recommended bleeding.

It was the customary treatment for all manner of maladies, and the prince, being the prince, received the best possible medical care, which meant that he was bled more. His doctors attached a belt of "thirty-six leeches around his waist" and then—after the leeches finally fell off, sated with royal blood—they moved him into a warm bath so that he would *continue* bleeding.

The prince lost over half a gallon of blood.

He survived.

There is no word on what happened to the leeches.

Presumably, they grew.

They would have been among the few things that did that year.

A VERY SHORT LIST OF WHAT GREW IN THE UNITED STATES IN 1816

Some rye. Some wheat. Some oats.

The vegetables that survived were lousy; the fruits were without flavor.

The corn crop—the foundation of a whole region—was an abject failure.

A nation of farmers looked at their fields and shuddered.

"No prospect of crops," wrote a pastor in Maine.

———◇———

But it was an excellent season for sparks.

A year of no rain on this side of the Atlantic meant that forests were parched, and in October, they went up in flames. The fires were impossible to fight: there were too many and the streams—the water that the firefighters would have used—were too low.

Maine burned first and its smoke drifted over all of New England. Bostonians did not have to leave the city to know that the country was on fire. They only had to look up. In Albany, looking up was not necessary. There had not been "a drop of moisture since June," a resident wrote, and now "the woods are everywhere on fire, and the smoke so thick" that the sun was blotted out.

New Hampshire burned. Vermont burned. New York burned.

Ferry captains on the rivers couldn't see downstream. They found their way through the smoke by compass.

Fiery cinders drifted through the air and fell on ships offshore.

They burned, too.

In a bizarre imitation of Tambora, the United States was dusted with ash.

———◇———

Fire was not the only growth industry.

Anxiety grew, too.

"This is beyond anything of the kind I have ever known," wrote a farmer in New Hampshire who'd habitually kept a diary of the weather. It was so extreme it was beyond record-keeping. "This past summer and fall have been so cold and miserable that I have from despair kept no account of the weather." The record would have been nothing but frost and drought.

The United States was still a new country. For decades, Europeans had claimed that North America had an inferior climate—that the land across the ocean was scarcely habitable. Its plants were less healthy, its animals smaller, its people weaker. These were racist, or at least deeply wrongheaded, ideas by Europeans who'd never left Europe. But they were the foundation of a debate that raged for years. Thomas Jefferson himself devoted many words to defending the American climate.

Now some Americans wondered if the Europeans were right. Even Jefferson was worried. "We have had the most extraordinary year of drought and cold ever known in the history of America," he wrote to a friend. The last year had been "the most adverse to agriculture which had ever been known."

The summer, concluded the *Niles' Weekly Register,* "has hitherto been extremely cold, with the exception of a very few days that were extremely warm." The *Register* feared that this was not an aberration, but a new reality. The climate was changing.

Would America become uninhabitable? Was this continent turning against its new inhabitants?

In Native American communities, the historical memory was long and the connection to the land deep. Here, there was no thought of leaving the land. The fight was to *keep* it. But the crisis was just as acute. A nation in New York State, part of the Iroquois Confederacy, normally harvested more than seven thousand bushels of corn.

In the Tambora year of 1816, it collected scarcely fifty.

SOME QUESTIONS FOR THE READER, ALSO KNOWN AS YOU, PART IV

Is that enough?

Enough information about the harvest, that is. Is it enough to establish that the year was catastrophic?

There's more. There's *so much more*.

Would more help?

———◆———

How much would be enough?

This isn't just a question about Tambora. It's a question that rings out hundreds of years after Tambora.

When do we have enough information? When do we believe something is really happening? When do we agree to move on to the *next* question—the question of what to do about it?

So although there's more to say about the harvest—the way people ate nothing but potatoes and salt for weeks, the way they ate porcupines, the way they ate animals designed not to be eaten—let's agree that we've said enough. Let's agree that something went horribly awry in the fields during these Tambora years.

And we will move on past the porcupines. We will move on to the pillaging.

BANDITS AND BLUDGEONS

ENGLAND AND EUROPE
1816

WHEN YOU DON'T HAVE BREAD, WHO'S AFRAID OF PRISON?

As the harvest passed without a harvest, prices rose yet higher.

For the poor, this was disastrous. For the elite, it was ominous.

Just south of London, a crowd demonstrated outside the home of a baker. The demonstration was peaceful until it wasn't. Windows were smashed. Things ended only when the demonstrators were threatened with prosecution under the Riot Act, which came with a punishment of death. It was a threat that worked.

But the authorities knew that the real problem was not the demonstrators. The real problem was the price of bread. If it kept increasing, the Riot Act would not be enough of a threat. The mayor of the town told the bakers: *Keep the prices under control.*

But in towns across England, the protests spread. Young men speared bread with sticks and smashed the windows of bakeries.

The authorities became more aggressive.

In Somerset, to the west of London, coal miners—some three thousand strong—went on strike. They wanted higher wages, they told the authorities, because they were starving.

The authorities were unmoved. The Riot Act was read. The militia was called in.

It attacked with "immense bludgeons."

———◇———

It was the poor who were protesting, but their poverty was not new. It was as old as time.

Across Europe, across Great Britain, the plight of the poor had always been grave. Sometimes it had been desperate. But before Tambora, they'd mostly suffered silently, inside whatever passed for shelter. They hadn't pleaded. They hadn't begged. They hadn't marched.

But this year—the year 1816—their lives had fallen apart so fast. Hundreds of thousands had begun the year with work, with food, with a roof. There wasn't much work, and there wasn't much food, and maybe the roof leaked. But they'd always made it before.

Suddenly, in this horrific year, it wasn't clear if they'd make it.

Their fragile existence had depended on a stable climate. A climate that did what it was supposed to do: sun and rain, at the right times, in the right measure.

A climate that was not stable, a climate that did not do

what it was supposed to do, a climate that went haywire—that was all it took to throw society into chaos.

A cloud of sulfates and ash, floating high above, had been enough.

———◇———

In France, bands of vagrants held up grain on the way to market. They demanded lower prices or the grain itself. They set fire to anything that would burn.

France had been through a revolution. Those in charge had seen this before. They didn't want to see it again. The government ordered that the price of bread in Paris be set. The price of bread would be like a centimeter, or a second: a fixed quantity, not something that went up or down. Paris was the largest city in France, and therefore the most important to keep quiet. A riot in Paris could turn into an insurrection in a very short time.

This order was not wholly successful—the cost of a loaf in Paris still rose, unlike a centimeter or a second—but it kept prices there lower than elsewhere. In fact, peasants came to Paris that winter precisely because prices were lower.

Which made Paris crowded with the destitute and the unemployed.

Which was the last thing the French government wanted.

In the countryside, the only hope was to go straight to the source. On moonless nights, groups of men went into the fields. They stripped clean whatever they found. Farmers hired guards to stand over their stunted crops.

In a village, residents overwhelmed the soldiers guarding the distribution of grain. Just a year earlier, in the Battle of Waterloo, the culminating battle of the Napoleonic Wars, these same soldiers had fought all of Europe at once. Now they were fighting their own citizens.

"Down with bayonets!" the crowd cried. They threw stones; they chased away the soldiers; they took city hall.

They took the grain.

The protests spread. They grew "like a fire." More city halls were sacked. Groups numbering in the thousands roamed the countryside, taking over towns, stopping grain shipments on the roads, raiding ships on the rivers.

"When you don't have any bread, who's afraid of prison?" shouted a protestor.

They were "spreading through the county, pillaging farms, besieging cities, not fearing to attack the cities or attacking troops and throwing them back." Sometimes the soldiers switched sides and stole the grain themselves.

Local officials could see which direction things were headed. They *joined* the protests. In the few areas with small surpluses of grain, officials refused to allow the grain to be shipped elsewhere in France. It was their grain, they proclaimed; it was staying right where it was.

Faced with a revolt in the countryside, on the eve of what looked like a dire winter, the government of France began to import large quantities of grain from anywhere it could be found.

———◇———

In November, the King of France, Louis XVIII, opened the legislative season.

"Tranquility reigns throughout the kingdom," he proclaimed.

This was untrue.

"My people suffer, and I suffer more than they do," he announced.

This was untrue.

In recognition of this suffering, the royal family would "make the same sacrifices this year as the last."

This was true.

They hadn't sacrificed then.

They wouldn't sacrifice now.

THESE GRUESOME FIGURES

A famine robs people of the ability to protest.

A revolution has to arrive *before* the famine. Once starvation nears, it is too late.

But if a starving person does not have the strength to protest, that person has a different sort of power: the power to shock. And all across Europe, the scope of the crisis was becoming shockingly clear. Those who were suffering looked "as if they had just crawled out of a crypt," an official wrote in what today is Germany. "These gruesome figures surprised and shook us, the plague on display at every turn."

This was but a preview. The coming year would be known in German as *das Hungerjahr.*

The Hunger Year.

It would be a year of people who desperately, urgently needed help.

The idea of *helping* was new.

Just a few years before, many philosophers had seen disasters as useful.

There were too many people in the world, they thought. There were especially too many poor people. If you could reduce the number of people, and especially the number of poor people, everyone would be better off, because there would be more food for those who were left.

Everyone would be better off—except the people who were reduced, that is.

(These philosophers were confident that *they* wouldn't be reduced.)

This is why after the disastrous Lisbon earthquake of 1755, the French philosopher Jean-Jacques Rousseau wrote that "it is quite a good thing that a certain number of people should get killed now and then." The English economist Thomas Malthus was less blunt, but he meant the same thing. Helping the poor, Malthus said, "relieves them for a short time, but leaves them afterwards in a condition worse than before." It was better just not to help at all.

Many believed it was impossible to help, anyway. The situation in 1816 was so grave, the Scottish philosopher James Mill wrote a friend, that no good could be done. "One third of the people must die—it would be a blessing to take them into the streets and highways, and cut their throats as we do with pigs."

So there was a bigger question than *how* to help. The question was *whether* to help.

Should the poor and the unlucky be left to suffer?

Should they be left to die?

THE BRIGHT SUN
WAS EXTINGUISH'D

SWITZERLAND
1816

IT WAS ON A DREARY NIGHT

It was July in Geneva, and July in Geneva was not living up to expectations, frankly.

"We have had lately," Lord Byron wrote in a letter at the close of the month, "such stupid mists—fogs—rains—and perpetual density."

He used the time inside well. He sat down on "a celebrated dark day, on which the fowls went to roost at noon, and the candles were lighted as at midnight," and he wrote a poem that would become immortal.

He titled it, appropriately, "Darkness."

The poem was a vision of an apocalyptic world, a world where "the bright sun was extinguish'd." It was a world of "desolation" in which "all hearts were chill'd into a selfish prayer for light." The achievements of civilization are undone. Sympathy fails. Selfishness prevails.

The poem begins: "I had a dream, which was not all a dream."

And indeed it was not. It was everyday life at Villa Diodati. The bright sun *had* been extinguished. Byron had somehow grasped the calamity unfolding around him. He'd seen the inhumane scale of climate change—its tragic cost. He'd seen that ultimately no one could escape its shadow.

That summer, it was easier to imagine a world of darkness than of light.

"What a thing it would be," Percy told Byron, gazing out over the Alps, "if all were involved in darkness at this moment, the sun and stars to go out. How terrible the idea!"

That summer, it was easier to imagine the sun going out than the sun shining.

When the year was over, the numbers were stark. During the growing season in Switzerland—the 152-day stretch between April and August—rain had fallen on 130 days.

Neither Percy nor Byron did well in captivity. On a rare day without rain, they left on a trip across Switzerland. They would sail.

With Percy and Byron gone, Mary sat down with her notebook:

It was on a dreary night of November, she began.

For the next week, she wrote furiously.

———◇———

On their journey, Percy came face to face with the consequences of the weather.

He'd been irritated. But now he saw that others were suffering far more than irritation.

"The children here appeared in an extraordinary way deformed and diseased," Percy wrote along the way. "Most of them were crooked, and with enlarged throats." These were the jarring signs of acute malnutrition. The residents of a village on the lake were "more wretched, diseased and poor, than I ever recollect to have seen."

After a week of traveling through the worst summer in Switzerland's history, Percy and Byron gave up. They were sick of the constant showers. They set sail for Villa Diodati, but the weather on Lake Geneva went from bad to dangerous. A sudden squall met their boat.

"The wind gradually increased in violence, until it blew tremendously," Percy wrote, "and, as it came from the remotest extremity of the lake, produced waves of a frightful height, and covered the whole surface with a chaos of foam."

The boat was close to some rocks, so Byron was in less danger. Byron could swim. But Percy was in grave danger. Percy could not swim at all.

Byron would not leave him. "My companion, an excellent swimmer, took off his coat," Percy wrote. "I did the same, and we sat with our arms crossed, every instant expecting to be swamped."

The pair gripped the sides of the boat, waiting for the end.

It did not come, not yet.

The boat stayed on top of the water. The squall subsided.

When they made it to shore, even locals wore "looks of wonder." Trees were toppled all along the shoreline, carved up by wind or lightning.

After taking the lives of so many, Tambora had spared Byron and Percy.

Afterward, Percy did not ask Byron for swimming lessons.

He did not learn that summer, or the summers that followed.

He should have.

———◆———

When Percy returned, Mary showed him what she'd written. He was enthralled. She should write more, he told her. This was not just an idea. This was a book.

Percy abandoned his ghost story. So did Byron.

Mary kept on.

Finally, though, she went outside.

She went to the Alps, along with Percy and Claire and a squirrel they adopted on the way. (In a shocking turn of events, it bit Mary's finger and was soon abandoned.)

On their hike up Mont Blanc, the highest peak in the Alps, they were almost victims of the shift in the seasons. "Suddenly we heard a sound as of a burst of smothered thunder rolling above," Percy wrote, "yet there was something earthly in the sound, that told us it could not be thunder."

Their guide pointed up. *Avalanche.*

In a normal year in Switzerland, avalanches fell in the spring, when the snow softened. But this year, the Alpine glaciers were expanding in the Tambora chill, and their shuddering sent avalanches down the mountainsides. They were still falling in August: "We saw the smoke of its path among the rocks and continued to hear at intervals the bursting of its fall."

Mary and Percy hiked to see the glacier that filled the valley. It was awesome and awful: it was "the most vivid image of desolation that it is possible to conceive," Percy wrote.

The central scene of her book, Mary decided, would be set there, on the glacier, the Mer de Glace. To Mary, it possessed a humbling, alien power. Its majesty and power made the affairs of humans look insignificant.

She did not know—she would never know—how wrong she was.

A CASTLE
ON A HILL

By the late summer, the money was running out.

Then again, the money was always running out.

This was life with Percy. There was family money, since Percy came from an aristocratic fortune, but it was tightly held by his father. Since Percy would never make any money himself—the thought was unthinkable—he was wholly dependent on what his father agreed to give him. He'd already taken out debts in anticipation of someday inheriting the fortune, but that money had run out, too.

Now Percy's father offered him more, but there was a catch: he must return to England.

So he and Mary and little William packed up. Claire would come, too.

Byron would not.

Byron would never see England again.

When Mary and Percy had originally eloped to Europe, a couple of years earlier, they had sailed back to England along the Rhine.

A voyage on the Rhine is famously picturesque. Cliffs shadow the river. Vineyards climb the slopes. Castles loom above.

At a break in the journey, Mary and Percy had stepped off their barge. Inland, they could glimpse a castle, or the outline of a castle at least, an impressive pile of stones.

Its name came from the ancient Germanic tribe of the Franks: *Franken.*

And it came from the German word for stone: *Stein.*

Franken. Stein.

As they left Switzerland this time, in 1816, as the party made their way back to England once more, this name may have passed through Mary's head again.

She had a book to write. And now she had a name.

Frankenstein.

By September, they were back in England.

Mary had just turned nineteen.

She was writing the great novel of catastrophe, a story of monstrous suffering.

And all around her, things were growing worse.

WHAT THEY ATE

FAR TOO MANY PLACES
1816

A CONTINENT
GROWLS WITH HUNGER

Some things bread was made out of in 1816:

Beets

Peas

Kohlrabi

Potatoes

Horse chestnuts

Moss

Lichen

Boiled grass

Straw

Bark

Cow skin

Sawdust

When there was enough wheat for bread, it was often wet wheat—the wheat that hadn't dried before harvest.

The wheat that moldered as soon as it was picked.

The wheat that arrived at the bakery half rotten.

Whole districts fell ill from moldy bread.

Even bread that wasn't rotten was inedible. Lousy wheat made lousy bread.

"You could not eat the bread," a French peasant said. "It stuck to the knife."

A recipe book for bread was published. The ingredients were mostly weeds.

"We should encourage the eating of old bread only," a newspaper in Bavaria suggested, "so that far less will be eaten because of the laboriousness of chewing."

Across Europe, grass was boiled.

Lichen was stripped off trees and eaten.

Cats went missing from whole villages. In Switzerland, authorities had to issue a warning telling residents it was not safe to eat cat *brains.*

When morning came, watchdogs were no longer on watch.

Were rats eaten? Rats were devoured.

Animals rotted, and then were eaten anyway.

People became vultures, scavengers of flesh.

"It is terrifying," wrote a Swiss priest in the town of Glarus, "to see these walking skeletons devour the most repulsive foods with such avidity: the corpses of livestock, stinking nettles— and to watch them fight with animals over scraps."

———◆———

And then they ate nothing.

In Switzerland, villages were decimated. Even the living, an observer said, had "the paleness of death in their cheeks."

———◆———

In part of what today is Hungary—in a region so isolated it took months for word of the crisis there to spread—tens of thousands starved.

In the hills of Italy, in the province of Lombardy, people survived, when they survived, on nothing but roots and herbs. Farther south, in Naples, the famine is considered the worst in history.

In Croatia, there was enough food to last six months, then enough food to last several months, then—then no food at all. "Reduced to the uttermost misery," a Croatian priest wrote of his parish, "they were walking around and falling dead, some at home, some along roads, some in the forests."

It was the worst famine in Europe since the 1600s.

The continent has never seen anything like it again.

———◇———

Those who did not die did not grow.

You can see it in the documents, the passport records: the average height goes down.

You can see it in the bones, in the skeleton of a Swiss woman who was an adolescent at the height of the famine. In the lines of her thigh, it is possible to see precisely when she suddenly stopped growing.

In the ice cores, we can see the volcano.

In the bones, we can see the famine.

That whole terrible volcanic decade, a continent shrank.

———◇———

In Scotland, the meteorologist George Mackenzie calculated the number of clear days—the number of *nice days*—in the first couple of decades of the 1800s.

The first decade averaged over twenty a year.

The second decade—the decade of ash and explosions—had under five.

It was a decade of damp shivering, with a handful of decent days a year. It was an awful time to try to get warm.

But there was one year far worse than the rest.

In 1816, George Mackenzie recorded no clear days at all.

———◇———

As the end of the year approached, a young clergyman in Austria—high in the mountains, cut off from the world—looked out at the world of snow around him.

Then he wrote "Silent Night."

Every time "Silent Night" is sung, there is an echo of Tambora: the weird weather, the weighty snows, the omnipresent fear of famine, the closeness of death. *Sleep in heavenly peace.*

"Silent Night" is a song of faith.

Faith was all there was left.

PART III

DREAD—JOHANN WOLFGANG VON GOETHE EATS
BREAKFAST—BUBONIC PLAGUE—A BAN ON WHITE
BREAD—STAMFORD RAFFLES VISITS FRANCE—BEGGARS
ON THE MARCH—WHAT NORMAL MEANS ANYWAY—
TO HELP OR NOT TO HELP—EVERYONE LEAVES
EVERYWHERE— THE SLEDDING WAS BETTER—A VERY
FUNNY SIGHT—A LIGHTNING STRIKE—A CREATURE—
SONGS OF REJOICING—A FLOP—A BOAT—A HEART

THE
DISTRESSING
DIN

EUROPE AND ENGLAND
WINTER AND SPRING, 1817

THE WALKING DEAD

The new year of 1817 was greeted with dread.

"Young and old usually celebrated on this day," wrote a Swiss observer, "but now there was an unusually hushed and solemn atmosphere everywhere; one heard only laments, and cries of woe evoked by the seriousness of the fearful times."

No one knew if the sun would shine. No one knew if there would be a harvest.

The farmers feared for their crops. The poor feared for their lives. The authorities feared for their authority.

If 1816 had been so bad, who knew how awful this year would be?

Who knew what would be left standing? Who knew *who* would be left standing?

No one knew what the year held, because no one knew why any of this was happening.

In February 1817, the German writer Johann Wolfgang von Goethe sat down to his newspaper. Goethe was and is the greatest writer in German history. But his mind had many corners and he was passionately interested in science and meteorology. He'd written poems inspired by Luke Howard's work on the clouds—he'd even written Howard fan mail.

The horrible weather plagued Goethe. His plans the previous year had been ruined by the "awful" skies. "It hinders everything good," he wrote. In the fall, he fell into a depression. "The uncertain days of fog and rain are by no means cheering."

And so when Goethe read the news that February morning, he was precisely the person who might see a connection where no one else saw anything at all. Few besides Goethe would be capable of fusing an eruption on the far side of the world with the skies outside.

"Newspapers," he noted in his diary on February 20. "Read the *Morgenblatt*. Story about a new volcano on Sumbawa."

The eruption had made Goethe's newspaper. It made his diary.

It sparked nothing.

Even Goethe could not imagine such a connection.

This year—1817—would be known as the Year of the Beggar.

In the words of someone who was there: "The people flowed through the towns and villages in droves, loudly crying out for the first necessity of life. The roads were filled with these unfortunates like armies on the march; market squares were their gathering places, entire streets were as if besieged."

The reaction was swift and brutal. Across Europe, begging was outlawed. Anyone caught was locked up in a workhouse. In Bavaria, beggars had a choice: whipping or jail. For multiple offenders, it was whipping *and* jail.

In many places, the goal was not to get rid of begging. The goal was to get rid of *beggars*. In France, there were hospitals where "people are herded together to get rid of them en masse through quick death from infectious diseases," said a German official. "Rome made use of the same method last year and in two days caused the horrendous number of beggars to disappear from the streets. They were penned up in their thousands like cattle."

———◇———

But they did not disappear altogether.

Across Europe, the dead were walking. Their bodies were skeletal, their eyes yellowed, their gait staggering. In Württemberg, a description went straight to the point: they "looked like cadavers."

Malnutrition makes the body ripe for disease. In Württemberg, smallpox broke out. In the Balkans, bubonic plague. In Switzerland, typhus arrived, taking out whole families at a time.

In Italy, it was pellagra, a disease of delirium. Pellagra only stalks the most malnourished, and in northern Italy, there was nothing but maize and millet, both new crops from abroad, both critically short of necessary vitamins.

Pellagra is deadly, and on the way to the grave it is cruel. It can make sufferers feel as if they are on fire from *within*.

In Italy, patients were so desperate to escape this feeling that they would leap into water even if they could not swim.

———◇———

The price of food was now unrecognizable. Like the ash of Tambora, it had gone into the stratosphere.

In some places, prices were so high and wages so low that people could work for a full day and still not afford a loaf of bread at the end of it.

The cost of basic foods doubled across Europe. But in parts of Germany and Austria—the soaked heart of Europe—prices would quintuple. In Switzerland, where white bread was banned—it squandered too much of the wheat berry—prices would eventually increase by a staggering 600 percent.

Since food was unaffordable, many seeking to survive went into debt.

But they had no way to pay it off—there was still no work.

And so the debt dragged them further under.

Remarkably, there was someone touring Europe that summer who'd breathed in the ashes of Tambora.

Stamford Raffles had commanded the British colony on Java. But his mission had failed, and Britain had given Java back to the Dutch. The island had not been a boon to the British, as Raffles had claimed it would be. In fact, it had been a hindrance, a "heavy burden on the finances" of the East India Company.

Raffles sailed home to England, but he was eager to see Europe, like so many Englishmen of the period. The wars were finally over; the sights could finally be seen.

What he found was not what he expected.

Raffles traveled with his cousin Thomas Raffles, who later published an account of their disappointments. Once they left Paris, they noticed "the almost total absence of life and activity" and "an air of gloom and desertion." They knew that the price of bread was high, but shielded by money and privilege, they hadn't registered the seriousness of the crisis, either in England or in France. But they soon found a population "in great distress." Beggars clung to their carriage: "They were chiefly children, and their number and their importunity were truly astonishing." The carriage was slowed by the steep hills and the children were able to walk alongside, "for a considerable distance," the whole time "entreating in the most piteous accents."

Sir

Please

Please give

Raffles and his brother were unmoved. "We were glad when a little level road allowed us to go on at a quick rate, and thus lose, for a while, the distressing din."

Stamford Raffles had borne witness to the cause and the effect—he'd seen Tambora and now he'd seen this distress half a world away.

He was surely among the very few people on Earth to bear witness to both.

He had no clue.

He did not—he could not—imagine the connection.

SOME QUESTIONS FOR THE READER, ALSO KNOWN AS YOU, PART V

Should there be more beggars here?

There are more beggars.

We can put in *a lot* more beggars.

———◇———

How many should we add?

How gruesome should the descriptions be?

There are descriptions that are easier to read and those that are harder to read.

Here's something easier:

To approach a village in Switzerland was to be "surrounded by one hundred unfortunates, as if blown in by a tempest."

Here's something harder:

"Children called out for bread; one could not refuse their small, entreating hands a bite of nourishment; old folk stumbled along half-decayed, like shadows of death . . ."

———◇———

Do those anecdotes help?

Help here means: Does it tell the story better?

It feels like it should. But it doesn't, does it?

More does not always equal *more*. Instead, all the stories pile up on top of each other. They merge into a single story. Their edge wears off; they grow dull.

Tragedy is just like anything else. After a while, it all starts to feel the *same*.

This book is about the consequences of Tambora—the consequences of a climate shock—which means talking about those consequences, and there are a lot of consequences. *So many consequences.*

But that has an unintended effect.

The more you hear about the fallout from Tambora, the *less* shocking it may feel. The more normal it may feel. A very weird sort of normal, a not-quite-normal sort of normal, but still: the word *normal* is in there.

It's easy to stop paying attention to what seems almost normal.

That's what normal is, after all.

Normal is what we call something that doesn't require attention.

It's true for the weather, too.

Maybe you have already felt that here—it would be hard *not* to feel it.

All those floods, all that rain, all those storms.

Another overflowing river.

Another early frost.

Another volcanic sunset.

The lousy crops, the lousy harvest, the lousy bread.

It all runs together, an exhausting litany of bad news. It's easy to stop noticing the badness.

But perhaps—pay attention to that *not noticing*.

Pay attention to that feeling that you don't need to pay attention.

Because if it is true for these Tambora years—this apocalyptic streak of bad weather—it might be true for ours, too.

SHOULD PEOPLE LIVE OR DIE?

EUROPE
1816 AND 1817

A SOUP OF THE DAY,
EVERY DAY

For those in power, there was still the haunting question about *whether* to help.

Should the poor and the unlucky be left to suffer? Should they be left to die?

In other words, should someone actually *do something*?

No one had good answers to these questions before Tambora.

Afterward, they did.

———◇———

The countries involved here have familiar names: England, France, the United States.

So they sound like the places we know.

They are not.

In the Tambora years, the United States had a very limited version of democracy: only white men could vote, and even then only if they owned a lot of property. But it was an expansive version compared to almost all of Europe.

A world in which most people have some say in what happens—that world did not exist then.

A few select people had a say. These were royalty, or wealthy landowners, or elites who'd risen to positions of power. The system protected their power, and it was why they were so worried about rebellion. Their job was to keep things the same. Their job was not to aid their citizens.

That was nowhere in the job description.

The citizens served the government. Whether the government served the citizens—well, that was a very different question.

———◇———

But Tambora posed that question.

And for the first time, many in power answered: *Yes*. They decided—more or less independently—to actually do something.

Since this was new—the whole doing something thing—they made it up as they went along. Mostly, they imported as much grain as they could find. The Russian Empire became the breadbasket for all of Europe, Odesa the port on which Europe depended. The grain came from farther away, too, as far off as Egypt.

Many towns founded a new type of aid organization, a sort of grain cooperative. The organizations, often funded by wealthy merchants, purchased grain directly from abroad, negotiated its passage, and sold it at drastically reduced prices.

These local merchants were the people closest to the need, and those who could see the need were often the first to help.

A wealthy Englishman was shocked by the sight of bedraggled men in the marketplace of a town outside London. They had been laborers in the hayfields, but there was no hay in the fields. Now they were "literally starving." The Englishman arranged for bread to be distributed—there was often bread to be had somewhere, if there was the money to afford it.

The first day, 140 men came.

The second, over 300.

The third, nearly 800.

And still they came.

———◇———

For a lot of Europe, national solutions were beside the point. Even the idea of the *nation* was still obscure.

People lived local lives. Many thought of themselves less as residents of a country than of a *place*—a village or a valley. In many areas, Europe was still a feudal land: the landowners held all the property and the rights; the peasants held none. The feudal system was ruthlessly exploitative. The peasants weren't supposed to make money, or advance in the world, or do anything besides *be peasants*.

But they weren't supposed to die of starvation, either.

So when the harvest failed, many landowners felt some responsibility for those who labored on their lands. You can see this in the account of a landowner in Moravia, today part of the Czech Republic. It was a time of calamity, he wrote. There were so many thousands in need that his private wealth was insufficient. "Now I am left with introducing a Rumford soup plan in order to save the majority of my dependents from starvation."

Rumford soup: barley, dried peas, potatoes, all boiled for hours and then poured over thin slices of bread. It was an innovation in social welfare, a dish designed to feed as many people as nutritiously as possible.

It was not designed for taste. There was salt, though. Count Rumford, who invented the soup—he really was called Count Rumford—was not a monster. He added salt.

This was the menu of the Tambora years, a single menu item, a single soup of the day, every day.

Millions of bowls were spooned out across Europe, across England, even in the United States.

It was part of this wholly new system of welfare—help the people who needed help. It was a revolutionary idea.

Even King Friedrich Wilhelm Karl of Württemberg—a man whose idea of charity was purchasing a rhinoceros for the royal zoo—even *he* did something.

His kingdom had royal storehouses of wheat, a sort of strategic food reserve for the elite. The king ordered that a portion of the wheat go to the poor.

Days after doing so, he died of gout, then a disease of royal excess and indulgence.

His son, who was wiser, got rid of the royal zoo altogether.

He pardoned anyone who'd stolen food out of hunger.

He funded aid for the poor.

Was all this aid out of generosity?

Was it out of humanity?

Was it out of caution?

Was it out of fear?

Was it *all* these impulses, all mixed up together?

Does it matter?

All we know is that after Tambora, there was an answer to the question: *Should someone do something?*

The answer was: *Yes.*

The next century would see a fierce fight over the role of government, and this new assumption would shape that fight. Did a government serve its citizens? Was a government responsible to its citizens? Did those citizens have a few fundamental rights—including the right to survival?

In the years after Tambora, these questions began to be answered.

A WORLD IN MOTION

THE RHINE
THE ATLANTIC
THE APPALACHIANS
1816 AND 1817

UP AND OVER
THE MOUNTAIN

All across Europe, people looked around and said the same thing:

Anywhere has to be better than this.

They packed up, if they were fortunate enough to have anything to pack, and they left.

They climbed mountains, they portaged rivers, they crossed borders.

Many in Europe tried to get down the Rhine to Amsterdam, where there were ships to America. But getting to Amsterdam took money, and often it took all the money these migrants had. They couldn't get farther and they couldn't stay in Amsterdam, either. Reports arrived of "whole multitudes of emigrants with their families, with an unbelievable number of small children" now forced to go *back* where they'd fled from.

Some never made it out of Amsterdam. An official from Württemberg was there: "Many parents die before their children, the poor, abandoned and helpless orphans wander around and must alas seek their bread at the doors of strangers. This misery is beyond words."

Even those who'd saved enough money to book passage to America were not safe.

In the middle of the Atlantic, a ship of Irish immigrants ran short of food. By the time the ship reached New Jersey, there was a famine on board. By the time the migrants reached Philadelphia, their destination, they were "so reduced to poverty and wretchedness that they were actually dying in the streets."

Those who survived found that the United States was not the refuge they'd imagined. After their extraordinary journey, they'd arrived in a place where people had the very same thought that had driven their own journey: *Anywhere has to be better than this.*

Tambora was not local. Tambora was global.

And since there's only one globe, somewhere better was hard to find.

———◇———

There was nowhere in the United States that felt like a safe bet. But there was somewhere that felt like a very bad one: New England. Across this stony region, people gave up and got out. They left without bothering to sell their farms. There were no buyers, anyway. New England was finished, many felt: a frozen, ruined land—a land without a future.

Sometimes this was literally true. After 1816, the town of Granby, Vermont, ceased to exist, vanishing from the map.

Everyone in Granby had left.

"A kind of despair seized upon some of the people," a New England resident wrote. "In the pressure of adversity, many persons lost their judgment, and thousands feared or felt that New England was destined, henceforth, to become part of the frigid zone." When his congregation looked ahead at another year in New England, a Connecticut minister wrote, all they saw was "a ration of baked potato and the bloodstains from bare feet in the winter snow."

In Maine, local newspapers ran letters to remind people how *great* Maine was.

There was less malaria!

It was closer to Europe!

The sledding was better!

In 1816, the growing season in Maine, always short, had been cut in half. It was scarcely a growing season at all.

It would take more than good sledding for people to forget that.

So many left New England that parts of the region would not recover for a generation.

———◇———

They all went west.

In 1816, the United States was still a nation huddled by the Atlantic.

But that was changing. Every year since the Revolutionary War, more settlers had crossed the Appalachians, heading west. They'd moved past the boundaries of the original colonies, and each new settlement brought more conflict with the Native Americans who were already there. In the War of 1812, many Native Americans, seeing an opportunity to preserve at least some of their homelands, had allied with the British. They'd fought desperately. But they'd been abandoned by the British, and the end of the war was a catastrophe for them.

Now, Tambora accelerated that catastrophe. In the coming years, waves of settlers, looking for better soil and weather, would force innumerable Native nations off their land.

"Old America seems to be breaking up and moving westward," noted Morris Birkbeck, who'd just emigrated from England himself. Wagon after wagon went west, each a mess of precious possessions. Those without wagons went by oxcarts; those without oxcarts went by handcarts. Whole families trudged west, walking up and over the mountains.

It was among the largest migrations in American history.

After a year of drought in America, here, finally, was a flood.

HOW TO MAKE A
MAN INTO A HORSE

The people were fleeing. But the animals were not. The animals were just dying.

And every horse that succumbed moved a community closer to famine.

Horses were the transportation of the day—any crops that did not go by river went by horse, and anything that went by river needed horses to *get* to the river.

Without horses, any harvest—what little there was—would not make its way to market.

From his waterlogged town in Germany, Karl von Drais saw all this. And then he changed the course of transportation itself.

The story of Karl von Drais is a barnacle on the story of Tambora—a little tangent, clinging to this narrative of ash and mud.

But these tangents matter. That's where the hope hides.

In 1785, a baby was born with the spectacularly unwieldy name of Karl Friedrich Christian Ludwig Freiherr Drais von Sauerbronn.

It was a name that suggested fame and wealth and glory.

Karl von Drais—for short—had little of any. He would make his own peculiar way.

He studied mathematics and physics, and then he acquired the sort of fantastic job that you could get in those days if you were a very clever, very minor noble.

A job with no actual work.

It was a job on paper—the chief forester of the Duchy of Baden—but the job in practice was to do whatever Karl von Drais felt like doing, and what he felt like doing was inventing. He'd been an inventor from a young age, and this was a golden age of invention. Among his creations: the earliest typewriter for recording shorthand, a form of note-taking; a meat grinder, possibly the original meat grinder; a hole-punching machine that transcribed piano music onto paper; and a periscope.

It's a dizzying list, and somewhere down it is something called a *Laufmaschine*.

June 12, 1817. Mannheim, a German city on the Rhine. The Rhine was swollen. The fields were waterlogged. The harvest was uncertain.

Amid all this dread, Karl von Drais arrived with an absurdity.

A *Laufmaschine,* he called it.

Or as the townspeople of Mannheim might have called it, a joke.

It had a pair of wheels, lined up one in front of the other, and a thin wooden board connecting them. The middle of that board was carved out and cushioned; this was the saddle, the seat. The front of the board had a sort of tiller that stuck out from the front wheel. By twisting this, a rider turned the wheel, navigating the roads like the helmsman on a ship.

Karl von Drais lifted his leg over the board. He leaned forward in the saddle.

And then he *ran.*

Laufmaschine is German for *running machine,* and that's what it was. A rider straddled the saddle, leaned forward against the armrest, and pushed off, the wheels carrying him forward. And then he pushed again. And then he pushed again.

The *Laufmaschine* was an "accelerator," Drais said. It took the effort of walking or running and it multiplied it. If a person was walking anyway, why not go faster with no more effort?

That day, Drais rode his *Laufmaschine* eight miles in less than an hour. This was fast, maybe three times as fast as a person could walk.

But he must have looked ridiculous.

We don't know how many people watched Drais that day.

We don't know how many laughed.

Every single one, would be a fair guess.

Today we look at the *Laufmaschine* and see it instantly for what it is.

A bicycle.

A very primitive bicycle. There was no chain on the *Laufmaschine*. There were no pedals.

But a bicycle all the same.

The idea was there all along. The technology was there all along. There's hardly any technology, actually: just two wheels and momentum.

It took Karl von Drais to see the possibility, because Drais saw its immediate use. A scaled-up *Laufmaschine* could solve the current crisis, Drais thought.

It could make a man into a horse.

The *Laufmaschine* was a stroke of genius, but it looked ludicrous. Drais would spend the next years traveling across Europe, exhibiting different versions of his machine. And something strange happened: his very practical invention became *fashionable*.

It was first popular in Paris, and then it crossed the English Channel and became a sensation in London. Soon there were hundreds of these machines on the streets there, where they became despised. This was partly because they were a shocking sight and partly because they were ridden so recklessly: accidents were common. The *Laufmaschine*s were now called velocipedes, but they were nicknamed dandy horses after the dandies who rode them: aristocratic men with nothing else to do.

This is where—inevitably—England's prince regent reenters the story. For the prince regent, the scandalous reputation of the velocipede was part of the appeal. The velocipedes were often seen on the grounds of the prince's estate, and at his birthday parties there was dandy horse racing.

Eventually, the craze died down. There were too many crashes, or at least too many stories about crashes.

The velocipede was banned.

Not just in London, but in America, too.

It would take decades before someone would look at the *Laufmaschine* and think: *Pedals.*

———◇———

All this happened too late. No one adopted the *Laufmaschine* in time to alleviate the hardship in the fields and the barns.

It's a classic story: a crisis reshapes the world and suddenly someone can see clearly what should be done. That's how new inventions emerge out of disaster: because the old way of doing things no longer works. But often the person with the invention is the *only* person who can see that far. Karl von Drais foresaw a new mode of transportation: with his running machine, he pushed himself out of the present and into the future. He could imagine a world in which getting around on two wheels and momentum was not shocking but normal. But no one else could see what he saw. They just laughed, because his *Laufmaschine* looked extremely funny.

This isn't just a problem for inventions. It's true for ideas, generally—for new ways of looking at the world.

It's something that Mary Godwin—soon to be Mary Shelley— was about to discover: when you see the world very differently from everyone else, other people might not be happy about it.

The best-case scenario might be that they'll laugh.

THE VERY BEST
OF INTENTIONS

ENGLAND
1817

SHE WOULD
NOT WASTE IT

As 1817 dawned, Mary was back in England, back in the country she'd so recently fled.

But she'd brought something with her from Switzerland: a novel, or at least the germ of a novel.

She was determined not to waste it.

She set to work. She wrote *Frankenstein* in a cottage on the river Thames, outside London. She wrote it while she got the news that Percy's wife, Harriet,

deep in despair, had killed herself. She wrote it while, a few months later, she and Percy married and she became Mary Shelley.

She wrote it in an absolutely freezing house.

It was freezing because the storms outside were relentless.

———◇———

Mary wrote *Frankenstein* while Percy wandered in the woods, giving away the few things they had. On a walk, he once gave away his shoes.

He came home barefoot.

People often lose their fervor as they age; Percy did not. As he grew older, his beliefs grew stronger. He would not sacrifice his ideals for a more comfortable life.

This was the man Mary had fallen in love with.

But still.

She wrote *Frankenstein* while she ran the house, on not enough money, while caring for their son, while pregnant with their daughter.

While Percy wandered in the back door, after dinner had been served, after the children were asleep, having spent the day drifting along in his rowboat, looking for inspiration among the branches overhead.

She wrote *Frankenstein* while Percy gave her clothes away to the poor.

She wrote it while Percy spent their money on live crawfish— not to eat, but to release back into the river.

Percy was a genius, and Mary made the allowances for him that people have always made for genius.

But she was also a genius, and no one made allowances for her.

She was still just nineteen. This is what she wrote.

A FEVER
DREAM

First, we need to clear up something. Contrary to popular belief, Frankenstein is not the name of the monster.

Frankenstein is the *scientist*.

Victor Frankenstein, native of Geneva, brilliant, young, driven by the thought that he—with the tools of modern science—could create life itself. He is good-hearted and gracious. He believes he is bettering the world.

He has the very best of intentions. But as Mary knew very well, intentions are not enough.

So if Frankenstein is the scientist, what's the name of the monster?

It has none.

The monster is outside society. Humans have names. The monster—the *thing*—doesn't have the dignity of a name.

Mary never calls it a monster, anyway.

She calls it a *creature*—a creature because it was *created*.

Let's use her term.

Because whether the creature is the true monster—or whether *we* are—that turns out to be a tricky question.

——◇——

Here's how the story goes:

Victor Frankenstein succeeds. In his laboratory, he jolts life into what was lifeless. But when he sets eyes on his creation, he's immediately horrified. He flees, tormented by the magnitude of what he's done.

It's too late. His creature is already alive. It is intelligent, kind, thoughtful. It is also an appalling, ghoulish sight. It is so repellent that it is instinctively rejected by everyone who sees it. It has no one to talk to, no one to love. Without any hope for the future, trapped in a society that despises it, the creature takes revenge on its creator, the person who brought it into this cursed world.

The creature happens upon a boy and then—discovering that the boy's name is Frankenstein—he kills the child, Victor Frankenstein's younger brother.

When the creature comes face to face with Victor Frankenstein, it is on the Mer de Glace, the forbidding glacier Mary had visited. Here, in this immense, inhuman landscape, the creature makes a demand: *I want a partner—I want someone to love. And in return, the two of us will quit this world and hide ourselves far away, never to be seen by humans again.*

Frankenstein is persuaded. But when he is about to bring this new being to life—he hesitates. In a fit of rage, he destroys it, ripping it apart.

And then the creature has its own fit of rage, and it is far more powerful.

It kills Frankenstein's best friend. It kills Frankenstein's bride.

It does not kill Frankenstein.

Instead, it torments him. It leads him on a wild chase, the creature ahead, Frankenstein always behind, desperate to find and destroy his creation, to save the world from more death.

To kill Frankenstein would be merciful: Frankenstein is already dead inside. The creature wants to keep him alive, to prolong his suffering.

Frankenstein will die, finally, when his body collapses, in the lifeless expanse of the Arctic, near the North Pole—the least human environment imaginable.

His creature will walk off into the blinding whiteness, never to be seen again.

SOME QUESTIONS FOR THE READER, ALSO KNOWN AS YOU, PART VI

What do you do with a story like *that*?

It's so relentless you have to exhale after even a summary, and any summary only undersells it. *Frankenstein* is far more scary. It's more profound, too. It's singular, a work of unearthly, piercing power. It reads like a fever dream, told by someone clinging to the edge of sanity.

But even with a thin summary, you can catch hold of its transfixing weirdness, its headlong descent into—well, into *something*.

What is that something?

Frankenstein has many meanings, and over the years, people have decided that it means many different things. It's about the horrors of the industrial revolution, or the failure of political systems, or the hollowness of humankind.

But there's something else there.

Frankenstein is a story straight out of the madness that Tambora made—a novel written from the epicenter of catastrophe.

There is the lightning, the constant lightning; there are the vicious storms.

There is the power of the creature, a power beyond reckoning—the power of a disaster.

There is its ugliness, the ugliness of the starving that summer, who—as Percy noted—were "deformed and diseased" and "crooked." Like the creature, the starving were a horror, a shocking sight. Like the creature, they deserved sympathy that they did not get. Like the creature, they had sunk below the status of human: they were something that should not exist.

Hunger distorts the body, stretches it, makes it repulsive.

A human becomes a *creature.*

This part of Frankenstein—this crisis that brought the story to life, just as Victor Frankenstein brought his creature to life—was long hidden.

It's not easy to see. It's been obscured by the past.

To glimpse it, we have had to travel through the wreckage of the Tambora years. We've needed the long perspective of history.

But we have our own perspective, too—the uneasy view-point of *now*.

And that might make it easier to see.

Because from the edge of one climate crisis, it is easier to recognize another.

BELLS AND SINGING

EUROPE
ENGLAND
THE UNITED STATES
HARVEST, 1817

A WORLD EXHALES

In the Tambora years, every season had been a mountain to climb.

That winter and spring—the first half of 1817—were no different. It was a long huddle against the cold and the storms. They were tight months, and the food was tight, too.

In Paris, smallpox deaths were still climbing.

In Belgium, a town aimed cannons at its own rioting population.

In Switzerland, Lake Constance swallowed whole villages.

But by that summer, there was a new feeling in the land. It was hope.

The prices were still rising, this was true. And the weather was still not great; no one called it great.

But they called it better.

And *better* was enough for a harvest.

High above, in the stratosphere where Tambora had settled, the air was clearing.

Even an eruption the scale of Tambora cannot stay aloft forever.

Gravity had gotten a grip. The many volcanic droplets had collided, forming heavier drops, and the extra weight was their downfall, literally. They drifted into the troposphere—the atmosphere fit for humans—and the currents there pulled them down to Earth.

It had been a long ride up there in the thin air—through 1815, and then 1816, and into 1817.

The weather of the 1810s was glacial. The world has never had a colder decade in recorded history.

But now the sun was coming out.

———◇———

In the United States, whole towns headed toward famine—and then skated around it.

There was no mass death. Corn and wheat had done horribly, but there were scarce grains and root vegetables—the sort of food that would survive the winter. Some vegetables were even helped by the weather: their habitual pests, canker worms and caterpillars, were killed by the frosts.

That spring, there was nothing to plant. The harvest in the fall had been so bare that few seeds were set aside, and there was no money to buy any—there never was. Seeds were not part of any budget. Seeds were saved.

Enough seeds were found that those without any cut a deal: for seeds now, they'd give up a part of the harvest later. They lost a little of their pride, but they survived.

They lived to see a harvest.

———◇———

When the wagons brought in the harvest, there were riotous celebrations.

Traditionally, the *last* harvest wagon had been celebrated—it marked the end of a long season of work.

231

Now, it was the first wagon that was greeted with joy—it marked the beginning of the season, the glorious fact that this year there would *be* a harvest. This year no one would starve, no one would walk the streets like the living dead, no one would eat bread made out of sawdust.

This year there would be food.

This year would be a good year.

In Europe, this reversal of tradition happened everywhere, and it happened spontaneously.

There were parades, flowers, bells, singing. There were speeches, so many speeches.

It happened even though the harvest of 1817 would have been a poor harvest in any other year. But after many months of barren, frozen fields, any harvest at all was regarded as a miracle. The soil had yielded its bounty once again.

The gratitude was so great—the *relief* so strong—that the celebrations became traditions. In towns across Europe, festivals arose that date back to this joyous harvest.

Some are still celebrated today.

———◆———

The relief must have been great among those who'd never suffered, too.

England's prince regent, Louis XVIII in France, all the assorted major and minor nobility of Europe: they'd survived, too.

They had all the trappings and levers of power, but that might not have been enough to make it through another year without a harvest. Their breakfast table would have been stocked, sure; they would always eat.

But that table might have been overturned.

The riots of the Tambora years had been put down. Sometimes the authorities had prosecuted those who'd dared to protest. Sometimes the authorities had quietly given in. It was a fragile balance, but it had held.

If the skies hadn't cleared, that balance wouldn't have held forever.

Rebellion had simmered. Given enough time, given enough scarcity, it likely would have boiled over. And even the wealthiest—the most powerful, the most secure—would have discovered that there was nowhere to run.

———◇———

Let us tick forward a year. By the summer of 1818, the sun had returned to London. There were nice days again. On his walks through the city, the meteorologist Luke Howard, who noticed everything, remarked on "the deeper green of the foliage and the richer colour of many flowers."

This was normal, of course. This was what the trees and flowers were supposed to look like.

Before Tambora, no one would have paid attention to such a thing.

Normal, after all, is what we call something that doesn't require attention.

NO ONE
IMAGINED IT
WAS MARY

ENGLAND
1818

DANGEROUS WATERS

Frankenstein was a flop.

No more than five hundred copies sold, a dismal number. It was called a "tissue of horrible and disgusting absurdity."

It was published anonymously, but Percy had written the introduction, and many people assumed he'd written the book as well. Percy was shocking, the book was shocking; therefore, Percy wrote the book.

No one imagined that it was Mary.

Perhaps her husband had written it. Perhaps her father had written it.

But Mary?

Anyone who bothered to read *Frankenstein* discovered that it was a stirring challenge to society. Mary knew this. She'd concealed her name, she wrote, out of "respect to those persons from whom I bear it." Mary was trying to protect her family.

She knew she was treading in dangerous waters, and she didn't want anyone near her to be swept away.

Mary was raised to be disobedient—to reason for herself, regardless of what others might say, regardless of what others might think.

Frankenstein is her magnum opus: it is a very disobedient book.

———◇———

By the end of *Frankenstein,* Victor Frankenstein is consumed with regret.

His ideas have not changed the world for the better, as his younger self imagined. His ideas have not been heroic. They have been horrific.

But he never realized it, not until the moment when it was too late.

Frankenstein is a nightmare, but the nightmare is not the creature.

It is us humans.

This is who Mary Shelley tells us we should be afraid of: *ourselves.* We catch ourselves in our own webs, woven of dreams and pursuits. We don't realize what we've done—what we've *created*—until it is too late.

———◇———

Shortly after *Frankenstein* was published, Mary crossed the English Channel, again. It was March 1818. She was bound for

Italy, and the voyage was rough, again. History repeats. They shuddered into France for the third time.

The party had grown. It was not just Percy and Mary and their son, William. It was also Clara, their six-month-old daughter. And not just Claire, Mary's sister, but Allegra, too—the daughter Claire had with Byron.

Out of this long list of passengers, only three would ever see England again.

Italy was warm, gloriously warm, but that warmth carried disease, and those diseases were new to the English travelers and they could be—especially to a young child—fatal.

Clara died in September, William the next June, Allegra a few years later.

For Mary, the pain was shattering. "The hopes of my life are bound up in him," she'd once said of William. After his death, she wrote: "Everything on earth has lost its interest to me."

But Mary was also pregnant, and a few months after William was lost, she gave birth to a new child. He was named after his father.

So much death, and then *this life*. How could Mary have faith that this child would live, knowing that the others had been lost so swiftly?

She must have seen the promise of death in his birth.

If so, she would have been wrong.

This child, young Percy, would live.

But the deaths were not done.

A few years later, the Shelleys were living on what is now known as the Italian Riviera—an impossibly beautiful stretch of coastline.

Percy had always loved sailing, and he had a new boat, designed for him by friends. After sailing to visit a friend along the coast, he set out for home.

A storm arose. The new boat did not do well, or Percy and his companions—there were two—did not do well handling it, or both.

Percy Shelley had never learned to swim.

The boat was found, washed up, days later. The bodies sometime after that.

Mary wrote, simply: "All was over—all was quiet now." Clara was gone, and now William, and now Percy. They were all gone. She wanted to go, too; she could not bear to be alive.

But a different Percy remained, and she had to stay with him.

She wrote: "Day after day I long only more and more to go where all I love are save my poor boy who chains me here—"

———◇———

In the decades after, Mary tried to salvage Percy's reputation.

He is now acclaimed as among the finest poets ever to write in the English language, but at the time his poetry and his ideas were mocked widely. Even Percy's father shunned Mary. He

gave her and young Percy—his own grandson—next to nothing to live on. He often refused her permission to publish new
editions of Percy Shelley's work.

His son could no longer be punished, but Mary could, and
she was.

Mary wrote stories for money. They were not intended to
be literary. They were not meant to last. They did not. But
somehow she would also publish a novel called *The Last Man,*
a visionary work of science fiction. It was overlooked upon
publication, just as *Frankenstein* was.

It is now a classic, just as *Frankenstein* is.

———◇———

After Mary's death, a box on her desk was opened.

Inside, wrapped in silk, was part of Percy's heart.

She was buried with it.

———◇———

Mary did not live to see what would happen to the Mer de Glace.

That was the "vast river of ice" that she'd hiked up in Switzerland. It was where she'd staged the fateful meeting between
Frankenstein and the creature.

The glacier was a setting as far from the affairs of humanity
as she could imagine—it humbled her and filled her with awe.
Victor Frankenstein regarded it with "something like joy."

But it was not far enough from the affairs of humanity.

The Mer de Glace is now melting away. It may be gone by the end of this century.

Written under the clouds of Tambora, *Frankenstein* is the product of climate change.

But Mary Shelley could not foresee how far that change would extend.

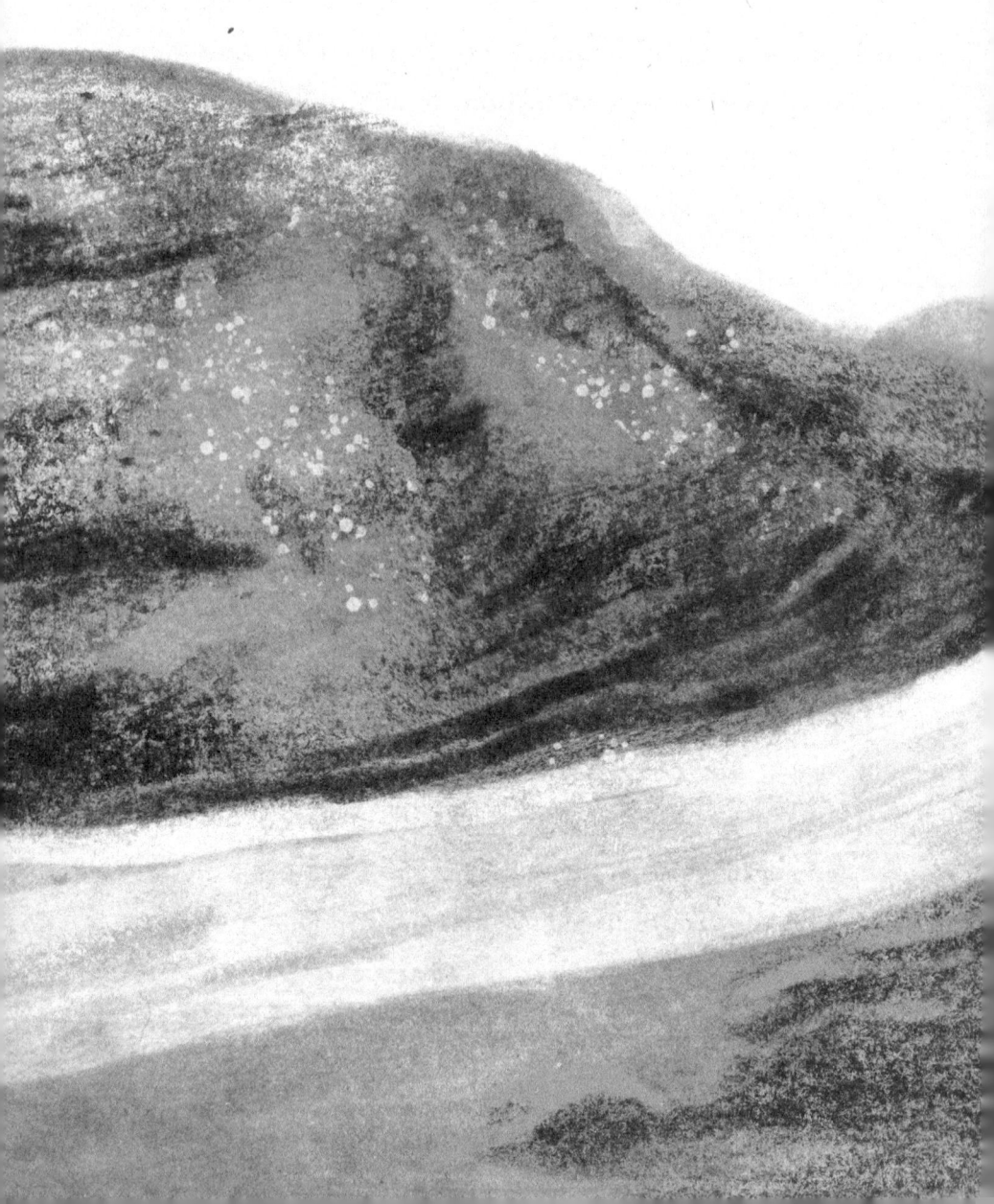

PART IV

DUST IN THE SKY—HUNGER STONES AND
MEDALLIONS—FINE CHINA AND PUMICE—DIGGING
BACK IN TIME—A QUESTION FOR YOUR AUTHOR
FOR ONCE—A CREATURE TO CHASE—A KERNEL OF
HOPE TO KEEP CLOSE—A CLOSING QUESTION

THE TIME OF
THE ASH RAIN

MOUNT TAMBORA, INDONESIA
TODAY

YOU HAVE TO IMAGINE IT ABLAZE

Tambora erupted more than a couple of centuries ago.

But the island of Sumbawa still bears the imprint of those terrible days, when the world was turned inside out.

Its once-fertile land is less profitable. Its residents are poorer than their neighbors. Malnutrition still plagues the island.

The beautiful coast was desolate for years. It was occupied again only many decades later, when the Sultan of Sumbawa sent slaves to live there—an eerie echo of those who died after Tambora *hoping* to be sold into slavery.

History has no shortage of cruel ironies.

—◆—

The land around Tambora is thick with what used to be inside the volcano.

It is all now inert, harmless.

So you have to imagine it in motion.

You have to imagine it falling from the sky.

You have to imagine it ablaze.

Because to dig here is to walk back through fire.

Underneath Tambora's soil is volcanic rock, what was once lava. Underneath that is the layer left by the pyroclastic flow—that river of hot gas and rock. This layer is thick, and past it is a sea of pumice, the lava blown skyward into bits of volcanic stone.

Underneath the pumice is ash, separated into layers. The layer from April 10, when Tambora erupted. The layer from the rumbling of the days before. The layer from April 5, when the trouble started.

The people on whom that deepest layer of ash fell—those people had no idea what was about to happen.

Archaeologists from Indonesia and the United States have now dug through all these layers. They have excavated a village buried by the eruption. They found fine china, perfectly preserved and still usable. They found jewelry made of precious stones. And they found people. Among them was a pair, a couple perhaps, once bone, now charcoal. The woman held a long knife. She'd been preparing dinner.

The archaeologists called the site the Pompeii of the East. They called it a Lost Kingdom.

But Sumbawans already knew well what happened. To them, it wasn't lost. They have their own name for those days:

Zaman hujan au.

The time of the ash rain.

A DISTORTION
FIELD

The Tambora years were a problem that fixed itself.

Suddenly, the sun shone like it should. Suddenly, the rain fell like it should.

Which was good, yes, it was great, but it was confusing, too. No one knew why it had happened. No one knew if it would happen again—next year, or maybe the year after.

The Tambora years were proof of how much depended on the weather. Everyone must have sensed that. But the weather was less dependable than ever.

So people decided to keep a wary eye on it.

The modern study of the weather was born in the years after Tambora. Shortly afterward, the United States set up a system for tracking and publishing weather data. Weather was no longer a curiosity. It was a matter of life and death.

In time, all this data would change the study of weather—

diaries of how much rain fell today—into the study of climate, the question of how weather works over time.

We know our climate is changing today—we are *able* to notice it—because Tambora changed how weather itself was seen.

———◇———

No one found the clues that Benjamin Franklin had left.

A century after Tambora, the meteorologist W. J. Humphreys published a paper linking volcanic eruptions with weather anomalies. (He published it, amusingly, in the *Journal of the Franklin Institute*.) Humphreys had a chart of average temperatures and a chart of volcanic eruptions. The lowest temperatures lined up with the dates immediately after the eruptions. It was not proof, but it was highly suggestive. The evidence would accumulate. It is now ironclad.

Still, even as late as the 1950s, sunspots were a central explanation. An academic paper from this time leads with sunspots, and only many paragraphs later does the author arrive at "another possible explanation" for the low temperatures: volcanic dust.

———◇———

Sunspots turn out to be caused by fluctuations in the magnetic field of the sun. These fluctuations make some areas more magnetic and darker, which we see as sunspots.

It turns out that sunspots do affect the amount of heat that the sun produces: they *increase* it. So there is a relationship between sunspots and how much heat reaches Earth, as many suspected. It's just the exact opposite of what everyone thought.

We also know that sunspots grow and shrink in a cycle, and that in 1816, they were at a low—there were *fewer* than usual.

No one would have believed this at the time, and for good reason. The sunspots were—well, they were *right there on the sun*. Even scientists who dismissed their importance could not dismiss their existence.

But it wasn't the sunspots that were different.

It was the *skies*.

The volcanic haze of Tambora had dimmed everything: the stars, the moon, the sun. And because the sun was dimmer, it was easier to see its spots. They weren't lost in its radiance. They were just—suddenly, shockingly, worryingly—*there*.

Even though they'd been there all along.

Tambora altered everything. In its haze, a person couldn't even trust what they saw with their own eyes.

———◇———

The memories of those years live on.

There are paintings of the suffering. There are memoirs written by those who suffered. There are stones memorializing the event, placed in public squares or on the walls of houses. Sometimes these document the record prices for wheat, or oats, or bread, as if it wouldn't be believed if it weren't written down.

There are medallions, struck to commemorate the famine,

with inscriptions like "Great is the distress, Oh Lord, have pity." There are memorials known as *Hungersteine,* or hunger stones. "Preserve us in future from the scarcity of famine times," one reads.

There are songs that can still be sung, and they are not happy songs: "Oh, the awful, awful time, Oh the great famine. First the long hardship of war, and now the dearness of bread! We scarcely saw such misery in years of war as oppresses us poor, poor folk in times of peace."

On the two hundredth anniversary of the *Laufmaschine,* Germany minted a silver twenty-euro coin with an engraving of Karl von Drais on his invention.

Behind him, in the far distance, is Tambora, erupting.

A QUESTION FOR THE READER, ALSO KNOWN AS YOU, AND THE AUTHOR, ALSO KNOWN AS ME

Many pages ago—before the floods, before the droughts, before the leeches—there was a part of this book that went like this:

The fallout from Tambora will land in the present—our today and our tomorrow.

We regret to say that this is your story, too. You're just like everyone else: you're stuck in a story you didn't even know you were in.

So it seems only fair to involve you.

But that left someone out.

I'm also stuck in this story.

So it seems only fair to involve me, too.

———◇———

Here's the question I have. It's the hardest question of all, which is why I saved it for last:

What does all this—this long voyage we've been on through the thunder and lightning of the past—what does it all *mean*?

It probably means *something,* after all. It'd be a little disappointing if we got all this way and then I was like: *Sometimes people don't get enough food and then they starve! Also, volcanoes are dangerous! That's all I've got here!*

Sometimes the author doesn't talk about what the book means. Or sometimes the author flat-out says what it is about.

But neither approach feels right here.

Because the story of Tambora and *Frankenstein* is a story about climate change and human folly—and what to do when suddenly the world goes very wrong.

And that's something we're all puzzling out together today.

That's why this is a question for *us*.

We ought to puzzle this out together, too.

OUR CREATURE

Our haywire climate today rhymes with the haywire climate of Tambora. Our story is a distant echo. There's the same unnerving realization that all life depends on a stable, predictable climate—and when that climate isn't stable or predictable, there's the same sense of alarm.

But there's a key difference: Tambora was a climate shock, and because it was shocking, it had a sort of twisted advantage.

It was fast. It was violent. People *noticed*.

The world is changing now, too, but in a very different way. Climate change today is sometimes fast and sometimes violent. But mostly it is slow. And mostly it is quiet.

Humans are very good at very many things.

But humans are not good at slow and quiet.

"Because we barely notice changes that happen gradually,"

the psychologist Daniel Gilbert writes, "we accept gradual changes that we would reject if they happened abruptly."

Tambora had another advantage, too. It just *ended*.

The chaos it caused continued to reverberate for years—the prolonged drought in parts of Africa, the still-not-right monsoon in India. But when the veil of ash and sulfates lifted, most of daily life down below went back to normal. The balance of sun and rain was largely restored. That's why it was so easy to forget about what had happened. The months of agony seemed like a blip, a freak anomaly. Besides, there wasn't any explanation for what happened, so there wasn't anything to do about it.

Anyway, that *just ending* thing that Tambora did—our story doesn't have that advantage, either.

———◇———

But it has a different advantage: people today know what's happening.

Since Tambora—in part *because* of Tambora—we've built an extraordinary infrastructure to understand the climate of our Earth. That's why we have so much information about how and why our climate is changing.

They didn't have any of this in the Tambora years. They didn't have weather forecasts, or even a science devoted to weather. Luke Howard had only just named the clouds, after all. They didn't have the foggiest sense of how the climate worked. (They didn't even understand *fog*.) They didn't have any way to grasp the larger forces that were shaping their lives.

That's why people ended up believing in prophets who told them that the world was ending. They didn't have a better story—a story built on knowledge and expertise—to believe in.

So people today have a huge advantage over those who lived through Tambora: we know *how* and *why* our world is changing.

How much of an advantage that is, though—that's unclear.

Because even after assembling this vast array of knowledge and expertise, it is still sometimes not enough. It's ignored, impugned, disputed, muddied, minimized, cast aside.

So just having this advantage isn't enough.

People have to trust this knowledge and expertise.

And then they have to *do* something with it.

———◇———

Like Tambora, *Frankenstein* was a warning.

Mary Shelley had a keen eye for the way we deceive ourselves. Victor Frankenstein is so convinced that he is doing good—he's so compelled by his heroic pursuits—that he can't see clearly. He thinks he's changed the world for the better, only to find out he's changed it for the worse.

Eerily, it is as if Mary Shelley were writing about *us today*.

After his creature is on the loose, Victor Frankenstein—the reasonable, good-hearted Victor Frankenstein—is haunted by what he's done. But he cannot unmake what he has made. It's too late. His creature is unbound.

The parallels are spooky. We've caught ourselves in our own web. Through the promise of progress, we have inadvertently created our own creature: the specter of climate change—the heat, the fires, the storms, the seas. We have created a creature that is no longer ours to control.

Suddenly, we are aware of what all our progress has wrought.

We are Frankenstein himself, chasing after our creature.

———◇———

While Mary Shelley was writing the great novel of catastrophe, people across the world were working in wholly new ways to *prevent* catastrophe. These were governments, and they were ordinary people, too. They were working on behalf of a simple idea, a new idea: that those who were suffering could survive— that they should survive—that they *deserved* to survive.

That there were things that could be done and should be done.

When we remember Tambora, what stands out is the bleak and the strange: the skeletal figures, the sawdust bread, the boils on the face of the sun. The disease. The distress.

But we should remember this part, too.

Without this idealistic work—without the invention of this idealistic idea—far more would have suffered. Far more would have perished.

Tambora was a warning.

But hidden inside it is this deeply hopeful truth: *we can act*.

A DELICATE, DANGEROUS LINE

Tambora is decapitated, but it is not safe. It is still classified as an active volcano. It may never erupt again, but it may never be safe, either.

It's not sleeping. It's napping.

The people of Sumbawa know this, of course.

They know it better than anyone. But there is nowhere on their island that is free from Tambora—this volcano that turned a green land gray, this volcano that for a brief period upended all expectations about how the world should work.

This volcano that unveiled a simple truth: that we are not the main character in our own lives—that everything we do turns on a stable, predicable climate.

But there is only so far those who live on Sumbawa can go. And so they walk a delicate, dangerous line: they live under Tambora, and because they do, they live as far from its peak as they can.

A FINAL QUESTION
FOR ALL OF US

Is it possible to live as far from Earth as we can?

ACKNOWLEDGMENTS

All the adjectives: Annie Kelley, who edited this book. Every author should be so lucky.

For her wisdom and good sense, Brenda Bowen. Thank you for making this journey such a pleasure.

For the wonderful illustrations that made this story come to life: Yas Imamura.

A huge thank you to Lee Wade and everyone at Random House Studio: Alison Kolani, Barbara Perris, Jessica White, and Debbie DeFord Minerva; Jade Rector and Tim Terhune; Katie Halata, Erica Stone, and Adrienne Waintraub; and everyone who's worked to put this book in the hands of children and librarians.

For research assistance: the librarians at Florence Lilly Library, Northampton Forbes Library, Smith College Library, the University of Connecticut Library, Amerika-Gedenkbibliothek in Berlin, and Staatsbibliothek zu Berlin. And Familiars Coffee and Tea.

So much love: Susan and Douglass Day, with a gratitude that somehow deepens with each passing year. Molly Peterson and Madeleine Day. David Kramer, Lina Bernstein, Ilya Bernstein. And closest to home, so close I can hear you as I type these words: the extraordinary Isaiah and Mila. I'll be right down.

And Anya. I don't care what the astronomical records say, there must have been a comet in the night sky.

BIBLIOGRAPHY

Abrams, Lewis J., and Haraldur Sigurdsson. "Characterization of Pyroclastic
    Fall and Flow Deposits from the 1815 Eruption of Tambora Volcano,
    Indonesia Using Ground-Penetrating Radar." *Journal of Volcanology and
    Geothermal Research* 161, no. 4 (April 2007): 352–361.

Bate, Jonathan. *The Song of the Earth.* Harvard University Press, 2002.

Behringer, Wolfgang. *Tambora and the Year Without a Summer: How a
    Volcano Plunged the World into Crisis.* Translated by Pamela Selwyn.
    Polity Press, 2019.

Behringer, Wolfgang, Christopher M. Clark, and Dorothee Wierling. *German
    History in Global and Transnational Perspective.* Edited by David Lederer.
    Palgrave Macmillan, 2017.

Bodenmann, Tom, Stefan Brönnimann, Gertrude Hirsch Hadorn, Tobias
    Krüger, and Helmut Weissert. "Perceiving, Explaining, and Observing
    Climatic Changes: An Historical Case Study of the 'Year Without a
    Summer' 1816." *Meteorologische Zeitschrift* 20, no. 6 (December 2011):
    577–87.

Boers, Bernice de Jong. "Mount Tambora in 1815: A Volcanic Eruption in
    Indonesia and Its Aftermath." *Indonesia* 60 (October 1995): 37–60.

Bosko, Natalia. "Exploration of the Sky: The Skies Sketchbook by J.M.W.
    Turner." *The Journal of the Royal Astronomical Society of Canada* 113,
    no. 4 (August 2019):138–150.

Brönnimann, Stefan, and Daniel Krämer. "Tambora and the 'Year Without a

Summer' of 1816. A Perspective on Earth and Human Systems Science."
Geographica Bernensia (2016).

Byron, George Gordon Byron, Baron. *Lord Byron: The Major Works*. Edited
by Jerome J. McGann. Oxford University Press, 2000.

Cao, Shuji, Yushang Li, and Bin Yang. "Mt. Tambora, Climatic Changes, and
China's Decline in the Nineteenth Century." *Journal of World History* 23,
no. 3 (2012): 587–607.

Chenoweth, Michael. "Ships' Logbooks and 'The Year Without a Summer.'"
Bulletin of the American Meteorological Society 77, no. 9 (1996):
2077–2093.

Clubbe, John. "The Tempest-toss'd Summer of 1816: Mary Shelley's
Frankenstein." *Byron Journal* 19 (1991): 26–40.

Collett, Anne, and Olivia Murphy, eds. *Romantic Climates: Literature and
Science in an Age of Catastrophe*. Palgrave Macmillan, 2019.

David, Saul. *Prince of Pleasure: The Prince of Wales and the Making of the
Regency*. Grove Press, 1998.

De Boer, Jelle Zeilinga, and Donald Theodore Sanders. *Volcanoes in Human
History: The Far-Reaching Effects of Major Eruptions*. Princeton
University Press, 2005.

Dippel, John Van Houten. *Eighteen Hundred and Froze to Death: The Impact
of America's First Climate Crisis*. Algora Publishing, 2015.

Donohue, Mark. "The Papuan Language of Tambora." *Oceanic Linguistics*
46, no. 2 (2007): 520–37.

Evans, Richard J. *The Pursuit of Power: Europe 1815–1914*. Penguin Books,
2017.

Fagan, Brian M. *The Little Ice Age: How Climate Made History 1300–1850*.
Basic Books, 2002.

Franklin, Benjamin. "Meteorological Imaginations and Conjectures."
Memoirs of the Literary and Philosophical Society of Manchester 2 (1789):
373–377.

"From the Java Government Gazette of May 20, 1815." *New York Evening Post*. February 27, 1816.

Gibbons, Ann. "Why 536 Was 'the Worst Year to Be Alive.'" *Science* 362, no. 6416: 733–734.

Goethals, Peter R. *Aspects of Local Government in a Sumbawan Village*. Equinox Pub, 2009.

Gordon, Charlotte. *Romantic Outlaws: The Extraordinary Lives of Mary Wollstonecraft & Mary Shelley*. Hutchinson, 2015.

Goulding, Christopher. "A Volcano's Voice at Eton: Percy Shelley, James Lind MD, and Global Climatology." *The Keats-Shelley Review* 17, no. 1 (2003): 34–41.

Hamblyn, Richard. *The Invention of Clouds: How an Amateur Meteorologist Forged the Language of the Skies*. Picador, 2001.

Hamblyn, Richard. *Terra: Tales of the Earth: Four Events That Changed the World*. Picador, 2009.

Hamlin, Christopher. *Cholera: The Biography*. Oxford University Press, 2009.

Harington, C. R., ed. *The Year Without a Summer: World Climate in 1816*. Canadian Museum of Nature, 1992.

Hay, Daisy. *Young Romantics: The Tangled Lives of English Poetry's Greatest Generation*. Farrar, Straus and Giroux, 2010.

Higgins, David. *British Romanticism, Climate Change, and the Anthropocene*. Palgrave McMillan, 2017.

Hitchcock, Michael J., and Roxana Waterson. "Short Notes: Is This Evidence for the Lost Kingdoms of Tambora?" *Indonesia Circle* 12, no. 33 (March 1984): 30–39.

Hitchcock, Susan Tyler. *Frankenstein: A Cultural History*. W. W. Norton, 2007.

Holland, Henry. "On the Pellagra, a Disease Prevailing in Lombardy." *Medico-Chirurgical Transactions* 8 (1817): 315–346.

Holmes, Richard. *The Age of Wonder: How the Romantic Generation Discovered the Beauty and Terror of Science*. Pantheon, 2008.

Holmes, Richard. *Shelley: The Pursuit.* E. P. Dutton & Co., 1975.

Hoppe, Andreas, ed. *Catastrophes: Views from Natural and Human Sciences.* Springer International Publishing, 2016.

Hoyt, Joseph B. "The Cold Summer of 1816." *Annals of the Association of American Geographers* 48, no 2 (June 1958): 118–131.

Hubbard, Zachary. "Paintings in the Year Without a Summer." *Philologia* 11, no. 1 (April 2019): 17–33.

Humphreys, W. J. "Volcanic Dust and Other Factors in the Production of Climatic Changes, and Their Possible Relation to Ice Ages." *Journal of the Franklin Institute* 176, no. 2 (August 1913): 131–60.

Johnston, Emma. "Up from the Ashes." *Popular Archeology* 7 (June 2012).

Jones, Pomroy. *Annals and Recollections of Oneida County.* Published by the author, 1851.

Klingaman, William K., and Nicholas P. Klingaman. *The Year Without Summer: 1816 and the Volcano That Darkened the World and Changed History.* St. Martin's Griffin, 2014.

Laskin, David. *Braving the Elements: The Stormy History of American Weather.* Doubleday, 1996.

Lebowitz, Rachel. *The Year of No Summer: A Reckoning.* Biblioasis, 2018.

Lessing, Hans-Erhard. "What Led to the Invention of the Early Bicycle?" *Cycle History* 11 (2001): 28–36.

Luterbacher, J., and C. Pfister. "The Year Without a Summer." *Nature Geoscience* 8, no. 4 (April 2015): 246–48.

Markley, Robert. "The Amherst Embassy in the Shadow of Tambora: Climate and Culture, 1816." In *Writing China,* edited by Peter J. Kitson and Robert Markley, 83–104. D. S. Brewer, 2016.

McCormick, Michael. "Climates of History, Histories of Climate: From History to Archaeoscience." *The Journal of Interdisciplinary History* 50, no. 1 (May 2019): 3–30.

McMichael, A. J., Alistair Woodward, and Cameron Muir. *Climate Change*

and the Health of Nations: Famines, Fevers, and the Fate of Populations.
Oxford University Press, 2017.

Millan, Laura. "Go See the Biggest Glacier in France Before It All but
Disappears." Bloomberg, November 17, 2020.

Munger, Michael Sean. "1816: 'The Mighty Operations of Nature': An
Environmental History of the Year Without a Summer." Master's thesis,
University of Oregon, 2012.

Munger, Michael Sean. "The Weather Watchers: Amateur Climatologists and
Environmental Consciousness, 1810–20." *History of Meteorology* 7 (2015).

Mussey, Barrows. "Yankee Chills, Ohio Fever." *The New England Quarterly*
22, no. 4 (December 1949): 435–451.

Officer, Charles, and Jake Page. *When the Planet Rages: Natural Disasters,
Global Warming, and the Future of the Earth.* Oxford University Press,
2009.

Oppenheimer, Clive. "Climatic, Environmental and Human Consequences
of the Largest Known Historic Eruption: Tambora Volcano (Indonesia)
1815." *Progress in Physical Geography: Earth and Environment* 27, no. 2
(June 2003): 230–59.

Oppenheimer, Clive. *Eruptions That Shook the World.* Cambridge University
Press, 2011.

The Parliamentary Debates from the Year 1803 to the Present Time. XXXIV,
Prince Regent Speeches (1816). 1283–86.
google.com/books/edition/The_Parliamentary_Debates_from_the_Year
/hXJGepkONvsC?hl=en&gbpv=0.

Peacock, A. J. *Bread or Blood: A Study of the Agrarian Riots in East Anglia in
1816.* Victor Gollancz, 1965.

Phillips, Bill. "Frankenstein and Mary Shelley's 'Wet Ungenial Summer.' "
Atlantis 28, no. 2 (December 2006): 59–68.

Post, John D. *The Last Great Subsistence Crisis in the Western World.* Johns
Hopkins University Press, 1977.

Prothero, Donald R. *When Humans Nearly Vanished: The Catastrophic Explosion of the Toba Volcano*. Smithsonian Books, 2018.

Raffles, Thomas. *Letters, During a Tour Through Some Parts of France, Savoy, Switzerland, Germany, and the Netherlands in the Summer of 1817*. Thomas Taylor, 1820.

Raffles, Thomas Stamford. *A History of Java*. 2 volumes. Black, Parbury, and Allen, 1817.

Robock, Alan. "Volcanic Eruptions and Climate." *Reviews of Geophysics* 38, no. 2 (May 2000): 191–219.

Rosen, Jody. *Two Wheels Good: The History and Mystery of the Bicycle*. Crown, 2022.

Ross, J. T. "Narrative of the Effects of the Eruption from the Tambora Mountain on the Island of Sumbawa on the 11th and 12th of April 1815, Communicated by the President of the Batavia Society." *Bataviaasch Genootschap van Kunsten en Wetenschappen* 8: 343–360.

Royal Institution of Great Britain. *The Journal of Science and the Arts*. Vol. 1. James Eastburn and Co., 1817.

Sampson, Fiona. *In Search of Mary Shelley*. Pegasus Books, 2018.

Scarth, Alwyn. *Vulcan's Fury: Man Against the Volcano*. Yale University Press, 1999.

Schoene-Harwood, Berthold. *Mary Shelley: Frankenstein*. Columbia University Press, 2000.

Schurer, Andrew P., Gabriele C. Hegerl, Jürg Luterbacher, Stefan Brönnimann, Tim Cowan, Simon F. B. Tett, Davide Zanchettin, and Claudia Timmreck. "Disentangling the Causes of the 1816 European Year Without a Summer." *Environmental Research Letters* 14, no. 9 (September 2019): 1–10.

Seymour, Miranda. *Mary Shelley*. Grove Press, 2000.

Shelley, Mary Wollstonecraft. *Frankenstein: Annotated for Scientists, Engineers, and Creators of All Kinds*. Edited by David H. Guston, Ed Finn, and Jason Scott Robert. MIT Press, 2017.

Shelley, Mary Wollstonecraft. *The Journals of Mary Shelley, 1814–1844*. Edited by Paula R. Feldman and Diana Scott-Kilvert. Oxford University Press, 1987.

Shelley, Mary Wollstonecraft. *The Letters of Mary W. Shelley*. Edited by Frederick L. Jones. University of Oklahoma Press, 1944.

Shelley, Mary Wollstonecraft. *The Novels and Selected Works of Mary Shelley*. 8 vols. Edited by Nora Crook, Pamela Clemit, and Betty T. Bennett. Routledge, 1996.

Shelley, Mary Wollstonecraft. *The Original Frankenstein*. Edited by Charles E. Robinson. Vintage, 2009.

Shelley, Percy Bysshe. *The Complete Works of Percy Bysshe Shelley: Correspondence*. Vol. 9. Edited by Roger Ingpen and Walter E. Peck. Ernest Benn, 1965.

Simond, Louis. *Switzerland: Or, a Journal of a Tour and Residence in that Country, in the Years 1817, 1818, and 1819*. Wells and Lilly, 1822.

Skeen, C. Edward. *1816: America Rising*. University of Kentucky Press, 2003.

Skeen, C. Edward. " 'The Year Without a Summer': A Historical View." *Journal of the Early Republic* 1, no. 1 (1981): 51.

Stoetman, Rik, and Dan McLerran. "Up from the Ashes: Discovering the Kingdom of Tambora." *Past Horizons*. November 2009.

Stommel, Henry M., and Elizabeth Stommel. *Volcano Weather: The Story of 1816, the Year Without a Summer*. Seven Seas Press, 1983.

Stothers, Richard B. "The Great Tambora Eruption in 1815 and Its Aftermath." *Science* 224, no. 4654 (Jun. 15, 1984): 1191–1198.

Tilly, Louise A. "The Food Riot as a Form of Political Conflict in France." *Journal of Interdisciplinary History* 2, no. 1 (1971): 23–57.

Vail, Jeffery. " 'The Bright Sun Was Extinguish'd': The Bologna Prophecy and Byron's 'Darkness.' " *The Wordsworth Circle* 28, no. 3 (Summer 1997): 183–92.

Veale, Lucy, and Georgina H. Endfield. "Situating 1816, the 'Year Without

Summer,' in the UK." *The Geographical Journal* 182, no. 4 (2016): 318–330.

Webb, Patrick. "Emergency Relief During Europe's Famine of 1817 Anticipated Crisis-Response Mechanisms of Today." *The Journal of Nutrition* 132, no. 7 (July 1, 2002): 2092S—2095S.

Witze, Alexandra. *Island on Fire: The Extraordinary Story of a Forgotten Volcano That Changed the World.* Pegasus Books, 2015.

Wood, Gillen D'Arcy. "Constable, Clouds, Climate Change." *The Wordsworth Circle* 38, no. 1–2 (January 2007): 25–33.

Wood, Gillen D'Arcy. *Tambora: The Eruption That Changed the World.* Princeton University Press, 2014.

Wood, Gillen D'Arcy. "The Volcano Lover: Climate, Colonialism, and the Slave Trade in Raffles's 'History of Java' (1817)." *Journal for Early Modern Cultural Studies* 8, no. 2 (2008): 33–55.

Wood, Gillen D'Arcy. "The Volcano That Spawned a Monster: Frankenstein and Climate Change." *Huntington Library Quarterly* 83, no. 4 (2020): 691–703.

NOTES

THE GODS WOULD RISE UP

He wrote back home: Wood, "The Volcano Lover," 37.

Raffles saw none of this: ibid., 40.

THE WORLD TURNED TO BURNING ASH

Sumbawa was small: Boers, "Mount Tambora in 1815," 39–40.

"Heavy guns," he noted: Royal Institution of Great Britain, *The Journal of Science and the Arts*, 251.

Troops were dispatched: Ross, "Narrative of the Effects of the Eruption," 343.

Vessels were sent: ibid.

The priests on Java: De Boer and Sanders, *Volcanoes in Human History*, 140.

A volcanologist once sought: Oppenheimer, *Eruptions that Shook the World*, 32–33.

"The whole mountain appeared": Ross, "Narrative of the Effects of the Eruption," 358.

The flames raged: ibid.

Then the stones: ibid., 358–359.

When Tambora erupted, the crew: Royal Institution of Great Britain, *The Journal of Science and the Arts*, 251.

"The darkness was so profound": ibid., 253.

When the ship could be seen again: ibid.

On top of the rock lay: ibid., 254.

"The sea was literally": ibid.

"The sound appeared": Ross, "Narrative of the Effects of the Eruption,"
343–344.

On the opposite side: ibid., 353.

Imagine a square: Klingaman and Klingaman, *The Year Without Summer*,
12.

When Stamford Raffles first arrived: For more on the slave trade in the region,
see Wood, "The Volcano Lover."

Its language was gone: For more on the lost language of Tambora, see
Donohue, "The Papuan Language of Tambora."

A decade after Tambora: Wood, *Tambora*, 17.

A NATURAL EXPERIMENT

Five years later, the seas: Boers, "Mount Tambora in 1815," 46.

Five years after *that*: ibid., 47.

The eruption had spared: ibid.

SOME QUESTIONS, PART I

How do you tell a story: I am indebted here to Wood, *Tambora*.

A COMET IN THE SKY

She was, he wrote: Sampson, *In Search of Mary Shelley*, 53.

A FEEDBACK LOOP OF BAD

We can still see: See generally Bosko, "Exploration of the Sky."

And it tells us about volcanoes: Wood, *Tambora*, 37–38.

IT WAS A SIGN

A German poet concluded: Behringer, *Tambora and the Year Without a
Summer*, 26–27.

It was "the heaviest": Klingaman and Klingaman, *The Year Without Summer*, 17.

The amount was not why: ibid.

Not a week into 1816: Wood, *Tambora*, 55.

The severity of the storms: ibid., 58.

Luke Howard did not know: Bodenmann et al., "Perceiving, Explaining, and Observing Climatic Changes," 583.

Bad weather was understood morally: Markley, "The Amherst Embassy in the Shadow of Tambora," 83.

THUNDER ROLLED DOWN THE YEAR

The waters were "washing": Veale and Endfield, "Situating 1816, the 'Year Without Summer', in the UK," 324.

By February, even families: ibid.

"Never," wrote an Englishman: ibid., 325.

By the time Tambora erupted: Klingaman and Klingaman, *The Year Without Summer*, 42–43.

"The rainy weather continues": Behringer, *Tambora and the Year Without a Summer*, 42.

Which is why the Alsatian: ibid.

In Germany a storm: ibid., 33.

SNOW AND SCANDAL

After weeks of this, Percy: Seymour, *Mary Shelley*, 98.

In the months that followed: Mary Shelley, *The Journals of Mary Shelley*, 69.

Mary dreamed that the baby: ibid., 70.

"The spring, as the inhabitants": Mary Shelley, *The Novels and Selected Works of Mary Shelley: Volume 8: Travel Writing*, 42.

"Never," she wrote later: ibid., 43.

WHAT IS TO BECOME OF THIS COUNTRY

It was a "full": "From the Java Government Gazette of May 20, 1815," *New York Evening Post*, February 27, 1816.

But in May, the ground: Hoyt, "The Cold Summer of 1816," 119.

"Everyone complains of the present": Klingaman and Klingaman, *The Year Without Summer*, 50.

"Probably no one living": ibid., 59.

From Maine: ibid., 66.

"Not a green leaf": Munger, "1816: 'The Mighty Operations of Nature,'" 49.

HOPES FELL FAST

Walking to work: Munger, "1816: 'The Mighty Operations of Nature,'" 1.

At the height of summer: Klingaman and Klingaman, *The Year Without Summer*, 158.

In Virginia, the frost: Skeen, *1816: America Rising*, 6–7.

THE FIRST WRONG

A French philosopher: Stommel and Stommel, *Volcano Weather*, 116.

"The philosophers assure us": Munger, "1816: 'The Mighty Operations of Nature,'" 28–29.

It was "at least worthy": ibid., 29.

The sun was said: Vail, "'The Bright Sun Was Extinguish'd,'" 185.

And by September: Klingaman and Klingaman, *The Year Without Summer*, 181.

They spread across the sphere: Vail, "'The Bright Sun Was Extinguish'd,'" 183.

The sun was sick: Klingaman and Klingaman, *The Year Without Summer*, 143.

If they did, the sun: ibid., 29.

"What agency the spots": Munger, "1816: 'The Mighty Operations of Nature,'" 30.

THE SECOND WRONG

And so in Germany and Switzerland: Brönnimann and Krämer, "Tambora and the 'Year Without a Summer' of 1816," 31.

AND A RIGHT

Its sagas sing: De Boer and Sanders, *Volcanoes in Human History*, 113.

But Iceland had never seen: For the full story of Laki, see Witze, *Island on Fire*.

In the words of an Icelandic pastor: De Boer and Sanders, *Volcanoes in Human History*, 121.

The smoky fog: Oppenheimer, *Eruptions That Shook the World*, 277.

The weather had been anomalous: Franklin, "Meteorological Imaginations and Conjectures," 375.

SOME QUESTIONS, PART III

William Herschel was the great: For this example, I am indebted to Munger, "1816: 'The Mighty Operations of Nature,'" 40.

CLAY AND CHOLERA

We know that Brazil: Chenoweth, "Ships' Logbooks and 'The Year Without a Summer,'" 2086.

We know that China: For the broader impact on China, see Cao et al., "Mt. Tambora, Climatic Changes, and China's Decline in the Nineteenth Century." For a full account of Yunnan, see Wood, *Tambora*, 97–120.

There was a "thick, 'heavy'": Behringer, *Tambora and the Year Without a Summer*, 23.

Whole regions: Harington, *The Year Without a Summer*, 538–40.

A deadly, disease-causing microbe: For the complete catastrophic details, see Wood, *Tambora*, 72–96.

Because cholera did not stop: For more on this apocalyptic outbreak, see Hamlin, *Cholera: A Biography*.

WE MUST HAVE FLOUR CHEAPER

In Germany, farmers were: Klingaman and Klingaman, *The Year Without Summer*, 114.

"During the entire season": Fagan, *The Little Ice Age*, 170.

The *Times* of London reported: Klingaman and Klingaman, *The Year Without Summer*, 112.

A more straightforward interpretation: Wood, *Tambora*, 65.

"Practically every means": Peacock, *Bread or Blood*, 26.

In a typical year: Post, *The Last Great Subsistence Crisis in the Western World*, 39.

They had a petition for the prince regent: Klingaman and Klingaman, *The Year Without Summer*, 108–109.

A protestor explained: Peacock, *Bread or Blood*, 79.

"So help me, God,": Post, *The Last Great Subsistence Crisis in the Western World*, 116.

The only remedy: *The Parliamentary Debates*, 1283.

First, he thanked the Parliament: ibid., 1284.

Only at the end: ibid., 1285.

The prince relied: ibid.

THIS EXTRAORDINARY TERROR

He'd come to a modest conclusion: Vail, " 'The Bright Sun Was Extinguish'd,' " 185.

The *Morning Chronicle* added: ibid.

In the English town of Bath: ibid., 186.

A maid in London: Munger, "1816: 'The Mighty Operations of Nature,' " 66.

In Liège, Belgium: Vail, " 'The Bright Sun Was Extinguish'd,' " 186.

Some "three-quarters": ibid.

"Suddenly cries, groans, tears": Klingaman and Klingaman, *The Year Without Summer*, 117.

The London *Times* wrote: ibid.

The London *Times* tried: ibid., 117–118.

In Paris the day before: Vail, " 'The Bright Sun Was Extinguish'd,' " 186.

Soon, a priest in Naples: ibid., 188.

The fear that: Wood, *Tambora*, 70.

A HIDEOUS PHANTASM

"I feel as happy": Mary Shelley, *The Novels and Selected Works of Mary Shelley: Volume 8: Travel Writing*, 44.

His carriage was designed: Gordon, *Romantic Outlaws*, 165.

"Unfortunately we do not": Mary Shelley, *The Novels and Selected Works of Mary Shelley: Volume 8: Travel Writing*, 45.

"The thunderstorms that visit us": ibid., 45.

"We often sat up in conversation": Mary Shelley, *The Journals of Mary Shelley*, 108.

"Perhaps a corpse would be reanimated": Mary Shelley, *The Original Frankenstein*, 441.

"One night we *enjoyed*": Mary Shelley, *The Novels and Selected Works of Mary Shelley: Volume 8: Travel Writing*, 45.

"*Have you thought of a story?*": Mary Shelley, *The Original Frankenstein*, 440.

She'd found the nightmare: ibid., 441.

I HAD THOUGHT OF A STORY

"The earth is so prodigiously": Clubbe, "The Tempest-toss'd Summer of 1816."

"I opened [my eyes] in terror": Mary Shelley, *The Original Frankenstein*, 441.

But she could not: ibid., 442.

"If I could only": ibid.

"I have found it!": ibid.

A VERY SHORT LIST OF WHAT GREW IN EUROPE IN 1816

By July, word came: Klingaman and Klingaman, *The Year Without Summer*, 114.

In August, a storm: ibid., 170.

It was a year: Veale and Endfield, "Situating 1816, the 'Year Without Summer,' in the UK," 325.

He was the king: Evans, *The Pursuit of Power*, 6.

Napoléon had once theorized: David, *Prince of Pleasure*, 200.

His doctors attached: Klingaman and Klingaman, *The Year Without Summer*, 171.

A VERY SHORT LIST OF WHAT GREW IN THE UNITED STATES IN 1816

"No prospect of crops": Klingaman and Klingaman, *The Year Without Summer*, 194.

There had not been "a drop": Munger, "1816: 'The Mighty Operations of Nature,'" 26.

"This is beyond anything": Laskin, *Braving the Elements*, 89.

"We have had the most extraordinary": Skeen, *1816: America Rising*, 1.

The last year had been: Klingaman and Klingaman, *The Year Without Summer*, 138.

The summer, concluded the *Niles' Weekly Register*: ibid., 153.

A nation in New York State: Post, *The Last Great Subsistence Crisis in the Western World*, 48.

WHEN YOU DON'T HAVE BREAD, WHO'S AFRAID OF PRISON?

It attacked with: Wood, *Tambora*, 61.

"Down with bayonets!": Stommel and Stommel, *Volcano Weather*, 50.

They grew "like a fire": ibid.

"When you don't have any bread": Tilly, "The Food Riot as a Form of Political Conflict in France," 54.

They were "spreading through": ibid., 55.

"Tranquility reigns throughout": Klingaman and Klingaman, *The Year Without Summer*, 229.

"My people suffer": ibid.

In recognition of this suffering: ibid.

THESE GRUESOME FIGURES

Those who were suffering: Behringer, *Tambora and the Year Without a Summer*, 54.

This is why after the disastrous: Webb, "Emergency Relief During Europe's Famine of 1817 Anticipated Crisis-Response Mechanisms of Today," 2092S.

Helping the poor: ibid.

"One third of the people": Klingaman and Klingaman, *The Year Without Summer*, 187.

IT WAS ON A DREARY NIGHT

"We have had lately": Bate, *The Song of the Earth*, 96.

He sat down on: Wood, *Tambora*, 66.

The poem was a vision: Byron, *Lord Byron: The Major Works*, 272.

It was a world of: ibid.

The poem begins: ibid.

"What a thing it would be": Klingaman and Klingaman, *The Year Without Summer*, 135.

With Percy and Byron gone: Mary Shelley, *The Original Frankenstein*, 22.

"The children here appeared": Percy Bysshe Shelley, *The Complete Works of Percy Bysshe Shelley*, 168.

The residents of a village: ibid., 169.

"The wind gradually increased": ibid., 171.

"My companion, an excellent swimmer": ibid.

When they made it to shore: ibid.

"Suddenly we heard a sound": ibid., 184.

They were still falling: ibid.

It was awesome and awful: ibid., 186.

A CASTLE ON A HILL

At a break in the journey: Seymour, *Mary Shelley*, 110.

A CONTINENT GROWLS WITH HUNGER

"You could not eat": Post, *The Last Great Subsistence Crisis in the Western World*, 41.

"We should encourage": Behringer, *Tambora and the Year Without a Summer*, 75.

"It is terrifying": Wood, *Tambora*, 63.

Even the living: Evans, *The Pursuit of Power*, 8.

"Reduced to the uttermost": ibid., 7.

In the lines of her thigh: Brönnimann and Krämer, "Tambora and the 'Year Without a Summer' of 1816," 33.

In Scotland, the meteorologist: Wood, *Tambora*, 39.

Then he wrote "Silent Night": Behringer, *Tambora and the Year Without a Summer*, 71.

THE WALKING DEAD

"Young and old usually": Behringer, *Tambora and the Year Without a Summer*, 73.

His plans the previous year: ibid., 38.

"It hinders everything good": ibid.

"The uncertain days of fog": ibid., 39.

"Newspapers," he noted: ibid.

In the words of someone: ibid., 54.

In France, there were hospitals: ibid., 56.

In Württemberg, a description: Post, *The Last Great Subsistence Crisis in the Western World*, 89–90.

In Italy, it was pellagra: Holland, "On the Pellagra."

In fact, it had been a hindrance: Klingaman and Klingaman, *The Year Without Summer*, 106.

Once they left Paris: Raffles, *Letters, During a Tour Through Some Parts of France, Savoy, Switzerland, Germany, and the Netherlands in the Summer of 1817*, 119.

But they soon found: ibid., 128.

Beggars clung to their carriage: ibid., 129.

The carriage was slowed: ibid.

Sir, Please, Please Give: ibid.

"We were glad when": ibid.

SOME QUESTIONS, PART V

To approach a village: Behringer, *Tambora and the Year Without a Summer*, 54.

"Children called out for bread": ibid.

A SOUP OF THE DAY, EVERY DAY

Now they were "literally starving": Klingaman and Klingaman, *The Year Without Summer*, 150.

"Now I am left": Post, *The Last Great Subsistence Crisis in the Western World*, 52.

The next century would see: For more on the broader ramifications, see Webb, "Emergency Relief During Europe's Famine of 1817 Anticipated Crisis-Response Mechanisms of Today."

UP AND OVER THE MOUNTAIN

Reports arrived of: Post, *The Last Great Subsistence Crisis in the Western World*, 102.

An official from Württemberg: Behringer, *Tambora and the Year Without a Summer*, 150.

By the time the migrants: Klingaman and Klingaman, *The Year Without Summer*, 193.

"A kind of despair": ibid., 245.

When his congregation: Dippel, *Eighteen Hundred and Froze to Death*, 43.

In Maine, local newspapers: Stommel and Stommel, *Volcano Weather*, 100.

"Old America seems to be": Behringer, *Tambora and the Year Without a Summer*, 153.

HOW TO MAKE A MAN INTO A HORSE

From his waterlogged town: For more on Drais, see Lessing, "What Led to the Invention of the Early Bicycle?"

The *Laufsmaschine* was an "accelerator": Rosen, *Two Wheels Good*, 28.

SOME QUESTIONS, PART VI

Frankenstein has many meanings: For a survey of its cultural significance, see Susan Tyler Hitchcock, *Frankenstein: A Cultural History*. For a critical guide, see Schoene-Harwood, *Mary Shelley: Frankenstein*. Note, however, that the latter volume skips over the ecological echoes in the text, as did almost all criticism until recently.

Frankenstein is a story straight out of the madness: For more on these remarkable connections, see Wood, *Tambora*, 64–66.

A WORLD EXHALES

The weather of the 1810s: Wood, *Tambora*, 39.

Traditionally, the *last* harvest wagon: Behringer, *Tambora and the Year Without a Summer*, 161–164.

By the summer of 1818: Wood, *Tambora*, 60.

DANGEROUS WATERS

It was called a "tissue": Seymour, *Mary Shelley*, 196.

She'd concealed her name: ibid.

Frankenstein is a nightmare: For more on this rich literature behind this idea,
see Mary Shelley, *Frankenstein: Annotated for Scientists, Engineers, and
Creators of All Kinds*.

"The hopes of my life": Mary Shelley, *The Letters of Mary W. Shelley*, 71.

After his death: ibid., 74.

Mary wrote, simply: ibid., 144.

She wrote: "Day after day": Mary Shelley, *The Letters of Mary W. Shelley*, 156.

That was the "vast river of ice": Mary Shelley, *The Original Frankenstein*,
121.

Viktor Frankenstein regarded it: ibid.

The Mer de Glace is now melting: Millan, "Go See the Biggest Glacier in
France Before It All but Disappears."

But Mary Shelley could not foresee: In fact, the dominant assumption at the
time was that the glaciers would ceaselessly expand and that the world
would be draped in ice. See Higgins, *British Romanticism, Climate Change,
and the Anthropocene*, 62.

YOU HAVE TO IMAGINE IT ABLAZE

But the island of Sumbawa: For a detailed ethnographic study, see Goethals,
Aspects of Local Government in a Sumbawan Village.

It was occupied again only: Oppenheimer, *Eruptions That Shook the World*,
311.

Archaeologists from Indonesia and the United States: See Abrams and
Sigurdsson, "Characterization of Pyroclastic Fall and Flow Deposits
from the 1815 Eruption of Tambora Volcano, Indonesia Using Ground-
Penetrating Radar."

Zaman hujan au: Boers, "Mount Tambora in 1815," 38.

A DISTORTION FIELD

Shortly afterward, the United States: Wood, *Tambora*, 227.

A century after Tambora, the meteorologist: See Humphreys,
   "Volcanic Dust and Other Factors in the Production of Climatic Changes,
   and Their Possible Relation to Ice Ages."

An academic paper from this time: Hoyt, "The Cold Summer of 1816," 130.

They were just—suddenly, shockingly: Munger, "1816: 'The Mighty
   Operations of Nature,'" 34–35.

There are medallions: Stommel and Stommel, *Volcano Weather*, 49.

"Preserve us in future": Behringer, *Tambora and the Year Without a Summer*,
   212.

There are songs: ibid., 213.

OUR CREATURE

"Because we barely notice changes": McMichael et al., *Climate Change and
   the Health of Nations*, 261.

Eerily, it is as if: For a reading of Frankenstein as a "climate change novel,"
   see Wood, "The Volcano That Spawned a Monster."

INDEX

Adams, John Quincy, 96
Africa, 112, 115, 259
Australia, 12, 125
Austria, 127, 179, 188
avalanches, 21, 169

Bangladesh, 114–115
Bavaria, 176, 187. *See also* Germany
begging, 187, 189–192
Belgium, 128, 229
Benares (ship), 10–11, 17, 25–26
bicycles. *See Laufmaschines*
Bima, 32. *See also* Sumbawa
Birkbeck, Morris, 208
Blake, William, 48
Bonaparte, Napoléon, 58, 68, 135, 146
Brazil, 112
bubonic plague, 188
Byron, Allegra, 239
Byron, Lord, 78, 134–139, 142, 165–168, 170, 239
    reputation of, 78, 134–135
    writings of, 78, 142, 165–166

charity. *See* social welfare
China, 112–113
cholera, 115
Clairmont, Claire (Jane), 48, 75, 77–78, 135, 169, 170, 239
    affair with Lord Byron of, 78, 135
climate shock, 6, 90, 111, 192, 258
clouds, classification of, 60–61, 259
Coleridge, Samuel Taylor, 49

comets, 48
Constable, John, 61
Croatia, 178
Czech Republic. *See* Moravia

dandy horses. *See Laufmaschines*
"Darkness" (Lord Byron poem), 165–166
Denmark, 119
Drais, Karl von, 209–214, 255

earthquakes, 45, 99–100, 101, 104, 107, 161
East India Company, 10, 25, 189
East Indies. *See* Indonesia
eclipses, 101
    volcanic, 29, 34
England. *See* Great Britain
Essay on the Modification of Clouds, 60–61

France, 67–68, 69, 78–79, 94–95, 101, 104–105, 115, 128, 129, 145–146, 187, 189, 213, 229, 232, 239.
    See also Napoleonic Wars
    protests and riots in, 157–159
Frankenstein
    climate change and, 242, 257, 260–261
    conception and writing of, 137–139, 141–142, 166, 168, 169, 217–219
    introduction of, 237
    meaning of, 220–225, 237–238, 241–242, 257, 260–261

Frankenstein (cont'd)
  origin of name of, 171
  publication of, 237–238, 241
Franklin, Benjamin, 97–98, 104–106,
  108, 253
French Revolution, 67, 125
Friedrich Wilhelm Karl of Württemberg
  (king), 146, 201

galvanism, 137
George III (English king), 66
Germany, 59, 68–69, 98, 101, 119, 145,
  150, 160, 186, 187, 188, 209, 210,
  255
Gilbert, Daniel, 258–259
Godwin, Mary. *See* Shelley, Mary
  Godwin
Godwin, William, 48–50, 76–77, 78, 142,
  233
Goethe, Johann Wolfgang von, 186
grain cooperatives, 198–199. *See also*
  social welfare
Great Britain, 45, 47–48, 54–55, 61–62,
  65–67, 69, 78, 96, 115, 119–125,
  127–128, 134, 136, 146, 156,
  170–171, 189, 197, 199, 200, 213,
  217, 233, 239. *See also* East India
  Company; Revolutionary War; War
  of 1812
  colonialism and, 10, 12–14,
    16–17, 30–31, 189
  Parliament of, 66–67, 125–126
  prince regent of, 66–67, 122, 126, 147,
    213, 232
  protests and riots in, 122–125, 155–156
Greenland. *See* ice cores, as climate
  record

Herschel, William, 107
horses, 15, 24, 30, 34, 79, 209, 212
Hôtel d'Angleterre, 75, 134, 135
Howard, Luke, 60–63, 186, 233, 259
Humphreys, W. J., 253
Hungary, 60, 177
Hungersteine, 255

ice cores, as climate record, 55–57, 61,
  178
Iceland, 103–105
India, 113–115, 259
Indonesia, 10–13, 39, 55, 103, 115, 250.
  See also Tambora
  colonization and, 12–13, 16–17, 189
  volcanic history of, 13–14
  industrialization, 88, 120–121, 223
Italy, 59–60, 67, 75, 101, 127, 128, 129,
  188, 238–240. *See also* Pompeii
  hunger and starvation in, 177, 187–188

Java, 10, 12, 17–18, 189. *See also*
  Indonesia
Java Government Gazette (newspaper), 83
Jefferson, Thomas, 150
Journal of the Franklin Institute, 253

Komodo dragons, 13
Krakatoa, 28–29

Laki, 103–106
Last Man, The, 241
Laufmaschines, 210–214, 255
lightning rods, 97–98, 99, 101, 106, 108
Louis XVIII (French king), 159, 232

Mackenzie, George, 178–179
magma, 9–10, 17, 20, 36
malaria, 13, 207
Malthus, Thomas, 161
Manchester Literary and Philosophical
  Society, 105, 108
Martinique, 21
Mayon, 57
Mer de Glace, 169, 222, 241–242
Mfecane, 112
migration and emigration, 112, 205–208
Mill, James, 161
Minoan eruption, 29
monsoons, 113–115, 259
Mont Blanc, 169
Moravia, 200
Morgenblatt (newspaper), 186

Morning Chronicle (London newspaper), 127
Mount Pelée, 21
Mount Vesuvius, 28–29, 251

Napoleonic Wars, 58, 68, 83, 101, 120, 158, 189
Native Americans, 150, 208
Netherlands, 12, 13, 16, 17, 189, 205
New York Evening Post (newspaper), 83
Niles' Weekly Register (newspaper), 150

Paine, Thomas, 48
pellagra, 188
Philippines, 12, 57
Philipps, Owen, 32
piracy, 16, 31
Pompeii, 28–29, 251
puerperal fever, 47
pyroclastic flow, 20–22, 250

Raffles, Stamford, 12–13, 17–18, 31, 189–190
Raffles, Thomas, 189–190
raja of Sanggar, 18–19, 24, 30
Revolutionary War, 83, 105, 208
rice, 19, 31, 101, 108, 112–113
Richter scale, 99
Rime of the Ancient Mariner, The, 49
Rousseau, Jean-Jacques, 161
Rumford soup, 200
Russia, 58, 111, 115
    as breadbasket of Europe, 198

Scotland, 161, 178. *See also* Great Britain
Shelley, Clara, 239, 240
Shelley, Eliza, 76
Shelley, Harriet, 76, 217–218
Shelley, Mary Godwin, 45–50, 69, 71, 75–79, 133, 136–142, 166, 168–171, 214, 217–222, 237–242, 260–261. *See also Frankenstein;* Switzerland
    anonymity of, 237–238
    appearance of, 49

birth of, 47–48
childhood of, 48–50, 142
children of, 75, 77, 218, 239, 240
death of, 241–242
elopement of, 77–78, 171
genius of, 49, 219
grief of, 239–240
other writings of, 241
return to England of, 170–171, 217
Shelley, Percy Bysshe (husband), 75–78, 133, 135, 139, 142, 166–171, 217–219, 224, 237, 239–241
    death of, 240–241
    finances and, 170, 240–241
    first marriage of, 76–77, 78, 217–218
    return to England of, 170
    swimming and, 168, 240
Shelley, Percy Florence (son), 239
Shelley, William, 75, 78, 218, 239
"Silent Night," 179
slavery, 16, 31, 113, 249
smallpox, 188, 229
social welfare, 161–162, 197–202, 261
sulfur, 36, 54, 99, 104, 141, 157, 259
Sumbawa, 10–11, 15–17, 27–32, 141, 186, 249–251, 262–263. *See also* Tambora
    destruction of, 29–31, 34–35
    horses of, 15, 24, 30, 34
    languages of, 11
    natural resources of, 15
sunspots, 93–96, 99, 100, 101, 107, 111, 119, 127, 129, 253–254
Switzerland, 46, 69, 71, 75, 78–79, 98, 119, 133–141, 146, 165–171, 185, 217, 229, 241
    hunger and starvation in, 177–178, 188, 191–192

Tambora, 11, 15, 16–17, 45, 50, 262–263. *See also* climate shock
    animal deaths caused by, 209
    apocalyptic prophecies following, 127–130

Tambora (cont'd)
   ash plume from eruption of,
      27–28, 35–37, 53–54, 157, 230
   collapse of, 27–28
   commemoration of suffering from,
      254–255
   death toll of eruption of, 32–33
   diseases spread by, 13, 115, 188, 207,
      229
   eruption of, 18–33, 53–55, 57, 59,
      249
   farming affected by, 67–68, 84, 113,
      119, 121–122, 145–146,
      148–152, 155–158, 185, 193,
      199, 229–232
   food prices affected by, 117,
      121–125, 155–158, 188–189,
      199, 229, 254
   hunger and starvation caused by, 112,
      160, 167, 175–178, 179,
      187–192, 199–201, 205–206,
      224, 230, 254–255
   migration caused by, 205–208
   newspaper story about, 83–84
   poem about, 32
   protests and riots following,
      122–125, 155–159, 233
   snowfall affected by, 59–60, 65, 67, 79,
      84, 85, 87–88, 113, 146, 179
   sounds of eruption of, 17–18, 25, 28
   sunsets affected by, 54–55, 193
   weather affected by, 6, 60–62,
      65–69, 79, 84–90, 93, 96,
      112–115, 119, 121, 129,
      136–137, 140–141, 145–150,
      165–168, 178–179, 186, 193,
      229, 232–233, 252
   wildfires and, 148–149
tectonic plates, 9–10, 11, 100
Times (London newspaper), 120,
   128–129
tsunamis, 29, 46
Turner, J. M. W., 54
typhus, 188

United States, 83–90, 91, 95, 96, 112,
   115, 148–150, 197–198, 200,
   205–208, 250, 252
   economy of, 88
   effects of Tambora on, 148–150, 230
   migration and, 205–208
   political system of, 197–198
   wildfires in, 148–149

velocipedes. *See Laufmaschines*
Villa Diodati, 136–137, 165–167
volcanic eclipses, 29, 34
Volcanic Explosivity Index (VEI), 28
Voltaire, 45

War of 1812, 83, 208
water cycle, 63
Waterloo, Battle of, 158
weather. *See also* lightning rods; Tambora
   as punishment, 63, 90
   science of, 63, 178, 182, 233, 252–253,
      259–260
Wollstonecraft, Mary, 47–48
Wordsworth, William, 48
workhouses, 121, 187
Württemberg, 146, 187–188, 201, 205.
   See also Germany

Yunnan province, 112–113